RALPH STORER is an expe[...] [...]vely
around the world. Despite [...] [...] in
Scotland since studying ps[...] [...]
great affinity for the Highl[...] [...]s
for a regular fix of nature, [...] [...]n-
fiction, and produces dark[...]

THE ULTIMATE
GUIDE TO THE
MUNROS series

THE ULTIMATE MOUNTAIN TRIVIA QUIZ CHALLENGE

BAFFIES' EASY MUNRO GUIDE series

A truly outstanding guidebook.
UNDISCOVERED SCOTLAND

Packed to bursting with concise information and route descriptions. There should be room for this guide in every couch potato's rucksack.
OUTDOOR WRITERS & PHOTOGRAPHERS GUILD

It is perfect for anyone exploring Scotland's beautiful mountains, whatever his or her level of experience. GUIDEPOST

THE JOY OF HILLWALKING

A treat for all hillwalkers active or chairbound. SCOTS INDEPENDENT

50 SHADES OF HILLWALKING

A fantastic celebration of this addictive pastime. DON CURRIE, SCOTLAND OUTDOORS

BY THE SAME AUTHOR:

100 Best Routes on Scottish Mountains (Little Brown)
50 Classic Routes on Scottish Mountains (Luath Press)
50 Best Routes on Skye and Raasay (Birlinn)
Exploring Scottish Hill Tracks (Little Brown)
The Ultimate Guide to the Munros series (Luath Press):
     Volume 1: Southern Highlands
     Volume 2: Central Highlands South (including Glen Coe)
     Volume 3: Central Highlands North (including Ben Nevis)
     Volume 4: Cairngorms South (including Lochnagar)
Baffies' Easy Munro Guide series (Luath Press):
     Volume 1: Southern Highlands
     Volume 2: Central Highlands
The Ultimate Mountain Trivia Quiz Challenge (Luath Press)
The Joy of Hillwalking (Luath Press)
50 Shades of Hillwalking (Luath Press)

Baffies' Easy Munro Guide

Volume 3: The Cairngorms
including Cairn Gorm and Lochnagar

RALPH STORER

Boot-tested and compiled by
Baffies, Entertainments Convenor
The Go-Take-a-Hike Mountaineering Club

Luath Press Limited

EDINBURGH

www.luath.co.uk

For Kay Sarah

First published 2015

ISBN: 978-1-910745-05-2

The paper used in this book is recyclable. It is made from low-chlorine pulps produced in a low-energy, low-emission manner from renewable forests.

Printed and bound by Bell and Bain Ltd., Glasgow

Typeset in Tahoma by Ralph Storer

All maps reproduced by permission of Ordnance Survey on behalf of HMSO. © Crown copyright 2010. All rights reserved. Ordnance Survey Licence number 100016659.

All photographs by the author.

CONTENTS

PREFACE

So you want to climb Munros but have understandable concerns that you may end up teetering precariously above an abysmal drop, sitting gingerly astride a knife-edge ridge or groping futilely for handfuls of grass on a crumbling rock ledge. If possible, you'd like to make it down to the foot of the mountain again. In one piece. Before dusk.

Let me introduce you to your new best friend: Baffies, the Entertainments Convenor of the Go-Take-a-Hike Mountaineering Club. In his club bio he lists himself as someone who is allergic to exertion, is prone to lassitude, suffers from altitude sickness above 600m, blisters easily and bleeds readily. However meagre your hillwalking credentials, if he can make it to the summit, so can you.

Our sister publication *The Ultimate Guide to the Munros* does what it says on the cover and describes routes of *all* kinds up *all* of the Munros. Not *all* of these are suitable for sensitive souls such as Baffies, hence the decision to 'delegate' him to write the guide-book you now hold in your hands.

When the club committee first suggested to him that he was the ideal person for the task, he almost choked on his triple chocolate layer cake. Only after we had managed to hold him down long enough to explain the book's remit did he come to embrace the idea. Indeed, he set about researching the contents with such a hitherto unseen fervour and thoroughness that we are proud to have the results associated with the club's name – a guidebook dedicated to finding easy ways up Munros.

Herein you will find easy walking routes up 25 Munros (and more!) – routes that require no rock climbing, no scrambling, no tightrope walking, no technical expertise whatsoever. Of course, hillwalking can never be a risk-free activity. No Munro is as easy to reach from an armchair as the TV remote. You will be expected to be able to put one foot in front of the other... and repeat.

Given that proviso, you will find no easier way to climb Munros than to follow in the footsteps of Baffies. I leave you in his capable hands.

Ralph Storer, President
Go-Take-a-Hike Mountaineering Clu

NTRODUCTION

OF MOUNTAINS AND MUNROS

It's a big place, the Scottish Highlands. It contains so many mountains that even resident hillwalkers struggle to climb them all in a lifetime. How many mountains? That depends...

If two summits 100m apart are separated by a shallow dip, do they constitute two mountains or one mountain with two tops? If the latter, then exactly how far apart do they have to be, and how deep does the intervening dip have to be, before they become two separate mountains?

Sir Hugh Munro (1856–1919), the third President of the Scottish Mountaineering Club, tackled this problem when he published his 'Tables of Heights over 3000 Feet' in the 1891 edition of the SMC Journal. Choosing the criterion of 3000ft in the imperial system of measurement as his cut-off point, he counted 283 separate Mountains and a further

255 Tops that were over 3000ft but not sufficiently separated from a Mountain to be considered separate Mountains themselves.

In a country with a highpoint of 4409ft (1344m) at the summit of Ben Nevis, the choice of 3000ft as a cut-off point is aesthetically justifiable and gives a satisfying number of Mountains. A metric cut-off point of 1000m (3280ft), giving a more humble 137 Mountains, has never captured the hillgoing public's imagination.

Unfortunately Sir Hugh omitted to leave to posterity the criteria he used to distinguish Mountains from Tops, and Tops from other highpoints over 3000ft. In his notes to the Tables he even broached the impossibility of ever making definitive distinctions. Consider, for example, the problem of differentiating between Mountains, Tops and other highpoints on the Cairngorm plateaus, where every knoll

At the summit of Lochnagar (R14)

Sir Hugh Munro himself never became a Munroist (someone who has climbed all the Munros). Of the Tables of the day, he climbed all but three: the Inaccessible Pinnacle (although that did not become a Munro until 1921), Carn an Fhidhleir and Carn Cloich-mhuilinn. The latter, which he was saving until last because it was close to his home, was ironically demoted to Top status in 1981.

surpasses 3000ft.

The Tables were a substantial achievement in an age when mapping of the Highlands was still rudimentary, but no sooner did they appear than their definitiveness become the subject of debate. In subsequent years Munro continued to fine-tune them, using new sources such as the Revised Six-inch Survey of the late 1890s. His notes formed the basis of a new edition of the Tables, published posthumously in 1921, which listed 276 separate Mountains (now known as Munros) and 267 Tops.

The 1921 edition also included J. Rooke Corbett's list of mountains with heights between 2500ft and 3000ft ('Corbetts'), and Percy Donald's list of hills in the Scottish Lowlands of 2000ft or over ('Donalds'). Corbett's test for a separate mountain was that it needed a re-ascent of 500ft (c150m) on all sides. Donald's test was more mathematical. A 'Donald' had to be 17 units from another one, where a unit was one twelfth of a mile (approx. one seventh of a kilometre) or one 50ft (approx. 15m) contour. Munro may well have used some similar formula concerning distance and height differential.

Over the years, various developments have conspired to prompt further amendments to the Tables, including metrication, improved surveying methods (most recently by satellite), and a desire on the part of each succeeding generation of editors to reduce what they have regarded as 'anomalies.' For example, the 'mountain range in miniature' of Beinn Eighe was awarded a second Munro in 1997 to redress the balance with similar but over-endowed multi-topped ridges such as the seven-Munro South Glen Shiel Ridge. Changes and the reasons for change are detailed individually in the main text (see Peak Fitness for details).

The first metric edition of the Tables in 1974 listed 279 Munros and 262 Tops. The 1981 edition listed 276 Munros and 240 Tops. The 1990 edition added an extra Munro. The 1997 edition listed 284 Munros and 227 Tops. Since then, following GPS satellite re-measurement , Sgurr nan Ceannaichean (2009) and Beinn a' Chlaidheimh (2012) have been demoted to Corbett status, leaving 282 Munros. Watch this space.

The first person to bag all the Munros may have been the Rev Archibald Robertson in 1901, although his notebooks bear no mention of him having climbed the Inaccessible Pinnacle and note that he gave up on Ben Wyvis to avoid a wetting.

The second Munroist was the Rev Ronald Burn, who additionally bagged all the Tops, in 1923, thus becoming the first 'Compleat Munroist' or Compleater. The third was James Parker, who additionally bagged all the Tops and Furths (the 3000ft summits of England, Wales and Ireland), in 1929. The latest edition of the Tables lists 1745 known Munroists.

THE SCOTTISH HIGHLANDS

The Scottish Highlands are characterised by a patchwork of mountains separated by deep glens, the result of glacial erosion in the distant past. On a global scale the mountains reach an insignificant height, topping out at (1344m/4409ft) on Ben Nevis. But in form they hold their own against any range in the world, many rising bold and beautiful from sea-level. For hillwalkers they have distinct advantages over higher mountain ranges: their height is ideal for day walks and glens give easy road access.

Moreover, the variety of mountain forms and landscapes is arguably greater than in any mountainous area of equivalent size. This is due to many factors, notably differing regional geology and the influence of the sea.

In an attempt to give some order to this complexity, the Highlands are traditionally divided into six regions, as detailed below. The potted overviews mislead in that they mask the variety within each region, ignore numerous exceptions to the rule and reflect road access as much as discernible regional boundaries, but they serve as introductory descriptions.

Broad Cairn summit (R11)

The Southern Highlands 46 Munros	Gentle, green and accessible, with scope for a great variety of mountain walks.
The Central Highlands 73 Munros	A combination of all the other regions, with some of the greatest rock faces in the country.
The Cairngorms 50 Munros	Great rolling plateaus, vast corries, remote mountain sanctuaries, sub-arctic ambience.
The Western Highlands 62 Munros	Dramatic landscapes, endless seascapes, narrow ridges, arrowhead peaks, rugged terrain.
The Northern Highlands 38 Munros	Massive, monolithic mountains rising out of a desolate, watery wilderness.
The Islands 13 Munros	Exquisite mountainscapes, knife-edge ridges, sky-high scrambling, maritime ambience.

THE CAIRNGORMS

The world-famous Cairngorms form the largest tract of high country in Britain, with more land over 1200m/4000ft, 900m/3000ft and 600m/2000ft (over 200 square miles of it) than anywhere else. Five of Britain's six highest mountains are found here – only Ben Nevis is higher.

To the north and east, the range is fringed by lower hills that run to the coastal plains of the North Sea. To the west, it is bounded by the A9, which runs north over Drumochter Pass to Aviemore and Inverness. To the south, the Angus glens descend to the Firth of Tay and the North Sea.

The Cairngorms National Park that was created in 2003 necessarily has a more limited perimeter than this traditional boundary, familiar to generations of hillwalkers. On its south side it originally stopped at the Cairnwell Pass on the A93, at the head of Glen Shee, thereby excluding a number of Munros south-west of there. In 2010 the southern perimeter was extended down to Blair Atholl on the A9 to include them. Some lobby to extend park boundaries still further.

Note that some Munros inside the park lie west of the A9 and are traditionally associated with the Central Highlands (Volume 2).

The Cairngorms have been known by this name for at least a couple of centuries and are named for their most

Summer snow in An Garbh Choire

accessible 4000ft mountain, which overlooks the resort town of Aviemore at the north end of the range. Ironically, the name means Blue Mountains, but in Gaelic they are Am Monadh Ruadh (*Am Monna Roo-a*, The Red Mountains), named for the pink colour of their granite. This contrasts with the mica-schists of Am Monadh Liath (*Am*

Let's get one thing straight: taking the easy way up a Munro does not diminish your hillwalking credentials. Just because you have your mind set on higher matters than groping rock all day doesn't mean you have to hang up your boots and go lie on a beach. The joys of hillwalking are not circumscribed by the difficulty of the endeavour. Sir Hugh himself was perfectly happy to take an easy way up a mountain if there was one and there's no reason you shouldn't follow in his footsteps.

Monna Lee-a, The Grey Mountains) on the other side of Aviemore across Strathspey.

On some maps the mountains are called the Grampians, but this elusive name has been applied so varyingly across the centuries that it has become meaningless. One OS map, for instance, places the name over the

Reindeer on Braeriach summit plateau (R20)

Northern Cairngorms, while another uses the name for all the mountains between east and west coasts.

Geologically, the primary Cairngorm rocks are igneous, crystallised out of magma. Most of the rock is coarse-grained and weathers into the grit that surfaces paths and produces excellent going, generally much better than elsewhere in the Highlands.

Ice Age glaciers have ground down the landscape's rough edges, leaving behind great plateaus topped by rounded summits. In places the weight of the ice has produced vast saucer-shaped depressions such as the Moine Mhor and the Moine Bhealaidh. More commonly the glaciers sliced through the plateaus to leave classic U-shaped glens, with hanging corries and huge rock walls, for the subsequent delectation of hillwalkers and climbers.

The region is divided into north and south by a great corridor that runs from west to east, beginning as Glen Feshie and ending as the Dee Valley. The Southern Cairngorms contain 32 Munros. The Northern Cairngorms contain the remaining 18, including the highest in the massif.

Of these 50 Munros, all of which are shown on the maps on the following pages, this guidebook describes easy routes up 25 of the most scenic (marked R1–R25). These include Cairn Gorm itself, mighty Ben Macdui (the second highest mountain in Scotland after Ben Nevis) and fabled Lochnagar above Balmoral.

If you reach all 25 summits you will come to know the Cairngorms intimately... and perhaps want to explore some of the more demanding Munros described in our sister series: *The Ultimate Guide to the Munros*.

As one explores them and wanders among them, the magnitude of everything begins to reveal itself, and one realises the immensity of the scale upon which the scene is set, and the greatness and dignity and calm of the Cairngorms cast their spell over the spirit.

From the first SMC guidebook by Henry Alexander (1928).

Memo to self: What are you waiting for? Get your boots on!

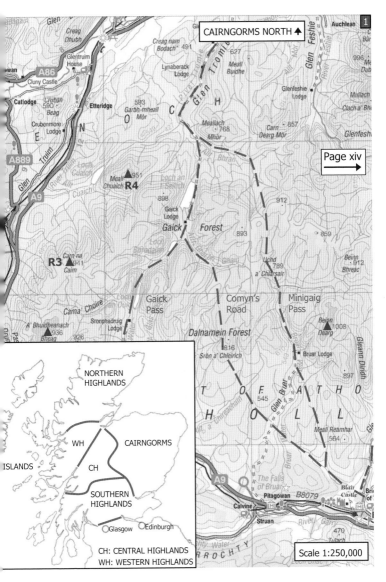

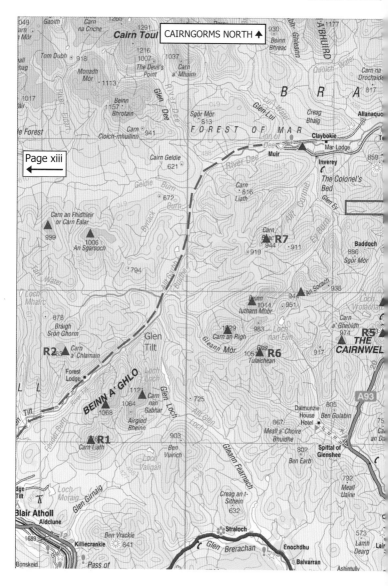

Page xiii ←

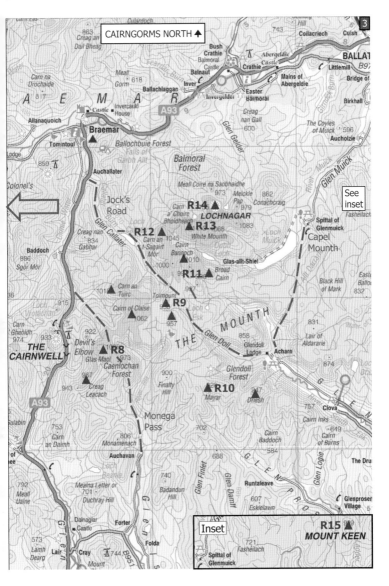

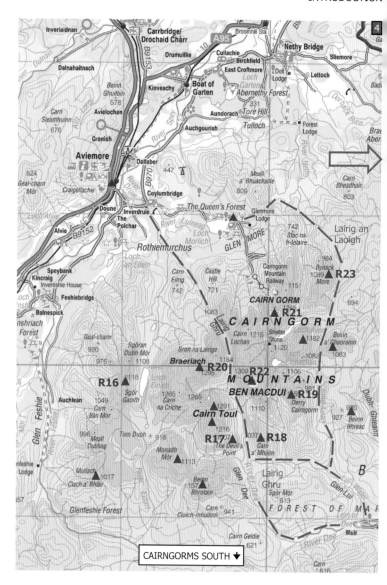

CAIRNGORMS SOUTH ↓

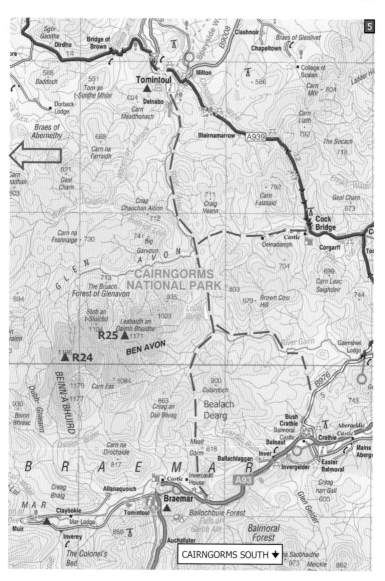

SEASONS AND WEATHER

From a hillwalking perspective, the Highland year has two seasons: the snow season and the no-snow season. The length of these seasons varies from year to year and from place to place.

From May to September, snow is rarely a problem. Historically, May and June have the greatest number of sunny days, with the air at its clearest. July and August are the hottest months but are also more prone to rain and haze, not to mention that blight on the landscape, the Highland midge. The biting season begins in mid to late June and lasts until the first chills of late September. By October it is colder, the hills get their first dusting of winter snow and good days are few and far between.

The months from November to April, though sometimes earlier and later, are characterised by short days, cold and snow. March and April are transition months, with little or lots of snow. In some years, snow can last into early summer and be a nuisance on some routes. If you are unequipped for it, turn back. Snow is more treacherous to descend than ascend, and spring snow often has a crystalline quality that makes it behave like ball-bearings.

In a normal winter (whatever that is, these days), conditions vary from British to Alpine to Arctic. An easy summer route can be made life-threatening by icy conditions and severe winter weather. When paths are obliterated by snow, hillsides become treacherous and walking becomes difficult and tiring.

On a clear winter's day the Scottish mountains have an Alpine quality that makes for unforgettable days out, but no-one should attempt a Munro in winter without adequate clothing and equipment (including ice-axe and crampons), and experience (or the company of an experienced person). The number of accidents, some of them fatal, that occur in the Highlands every winter should leave no doubt as to the need for caution.

Battling a gale on Carn Liath (R1)

Sample weather forecasts:
www.metoffice.gov.uk/public/weather/
    mountain-forecast
www.metcheck.com/HOBBIES/
    mountain.asp
www.mwis.org.uk
www.sais.gov.uk (avalanche conditions)

Useful webcams at the time of writing can be found at:
    www.ski-glenshee.co.uk
    www.cairngormmountain.org
    www.snoweye.com/?resort=uk_glenshee
    www.snoweye.com/?resort=
    uk_cairngorm

USING THIS BOOK

Position in Munro's Tables
(1 = highest)

OS 1:50,000
map number

Grid reference

▲ **Glas Tulaichean** 79 1051/3448ft (OS 43, NO 051760)
Glass Toolichan, Green Knolls

Many Munro names are Gaelic in origin. We give approximate pronunciations but make no claim to definitiveness. For example, the correct pronunciation of Ben is akin to *Pyne*, with a soft *n* as in the first syllable of *onion*, but it would be pedantic to enforce a purist pronunciation on a non-Gaelic speaker. The name Bealach, meaning Pass, is pronounced *byalach*, but many find it hard not to call it a *beelach*. And if you're one of those unfortunates who appear congenitally incapable of pronouncing *loch* as anything other than *lock*, you're in trouble.

In connection with the phonetic pronunciations given, note that Y before a vowel is pronounced as in *you*, OW is pronounced as in *town* and CH is pronounced as in Scottish *loch* or German *noch*.

Tolmount from Glen Clova via Jock's Road
NO 284762, 12ml/19km, 770m/2500ft

The maps used in this book are reproductions of OS 1:50,000 maps at 75% full size (i.e. 1:66,667 or 1.5cm per 1km).

Route distances are specified in miles (to the nearest half-mile) and kilometres (to the nearest kilometre). Short distances are specified in metres (an approximate imperial measurement is yards). Total amount of ascent for a route is specified to the nearest 10m (50ft) and should be regarded as an approximation only.

To calculate how long a route will take, many begin with Naismith's Rule (one hour per 3ml/5km + half-hour per 1000ft/300m). This can be adjusted by an appropriate factor to suit your own pace and to cater for stoppages, foul weather, technical difficulty, rough terrain, tiredness and decrepitude. (Bill Naismith, 1856–1935, was the 'father' of the SMC.)

River directions, left bank and right bank, refer to the downstream direction. When referring to the direction of travel, we specify left-hand and right-hand.

The symbols ▲ and Δ indicate Munros and Tops. An ATV track is an All-Terrain Vehicle track, rougher than a Land Rover track.

ACCESS

L and access was revolutionised by The Land Reform (Scotland) Act 2003 and the accompanying Scottish Outdoor Access Code (2005), which created a statutory right of responsible access for outdoor recreation. It is recommended that anyone walking in the Scottish countryside familiarise himself/herself with the Code, which explains rights and responsibilities in detail. Further information: www.outdooraccess-scotland.com.

Deer stalking considerations: Despite the fact that all the Munros in this volume fall within the boundaries of the Cairngorms National Park, most of the land is privately owned and access may be restricted in certain places during the stalking season. Non-compliance with restrictions is likely to cause aggravation for all concerned. If revenue is lost because of interference with stalking activities, estates may be forced to turn to afforestation or worse, thereby increasing access problems. Note that there is no stalking on a Sunday.

The red stag stalking season runs from July 1 to October 20 but actual dates vary from locality to locality. Access notices dot the roadside and information on stalking activities can be obtained from estate offices and head stalkers. Specific information given in the main text is subject to change and should be verified.

An increasing number of estates contribute to the 'Heading for the Scottish Hills' service, which provides daily details of where stalking is taking place. Further information can be found on the Outdoor Access website: www.outdooraccess-scotland.com/hftsh.

The good news is that there are no access restrictions at any time of year if you stick to the main routes described in this guidebook.

TERRAIN

T hanks to the generally peat-free granite bedrock and the proliferation of vehicle tracks and renovated paths, the Cairngorms have the best hiking terrain in the Scottish Highlands. However, good going is not to be relied upon everywhere. Boggy ground is commonplace on the great mosses (Moine Mhor and Moine Bhealaidh) and elsewhere. In other places, notably on the plateaus and at the summits, rockier terrain precludes the formation of any path.

In general, be prepared always for rough, rugged terrain and wear appropriate footwear.

The Carn Ban Mor path (R16)

Beinn a' Ghlo: *Ben a Glaw*, Veiled Mountain or Mountain of Mist

▲ **Carn Liath** 181 975m/3199ft (OS 43, NN 936698)

Carn Lee-a, Grey Cairn, named for its summit screes

▲ **Braigh Coire Chruinn-bhalgain** 66
1070m/3510ft (OS 43, NN 945724) *Bry Corra Croo-in Valagin*,
Upland of the Corrie of Round Blisters

▲ **Carn nan Gabhar** 32 1121m/3678ft (OS 43, NN 971733)
Carn nan Gower, Goat Cairn

CARN LIATH — BRAIGH COIRE CHRUINN-BHALGAIN — Airgiod Bheinn — CARN NAN GABHAR

Beinn a' Ghlo from Ben Vrackie above Pitlochry

Isolated by deep glens on all sides, the Beinn a' Ghlo massif has been carved by a confusion of corries into a multi-faceted miniature mountain range of great character. Famously, according to an old stalkers' legend, there are 19 corries, all so distinct that a rifle can be fired in any without being heard in another.

Steep hillsides of grass, heather and scree support three distinct Munros on a twisting main ridge that runs from south to north parallel to Glen Tilt.

The three Munros are strung out in a line above the glen, but the closure of the road to the public (see Page 6) has made a long approach walk necessary from this side.

Fortunately, another road climbs to a height of 340m/1100ft near the foot of Carn Liath, the first Munro. The high starting point, short approach walk and directissima ascent path put the summit within easy reach, and the over-fit can optionally extend the route to bag the other two Munros.

The Beinn a' Ghlo Munros stand at the very edge of the Highlands and command a vista that extends southwards as far as Edinburgh's Pentland Hills some eighty miles away.

Carn Liath from Loch Moraig near Blair Atholl
NN 906671, 6ml/10km, 640m/2100ft

CARN LIATH   The approach track in winter

From Blair Atholl, take the minor road to Loch Moraig. Park by the roadside at the end of the public road and walk along the continuing private road to Monzie farm. When the road bends left to the farm after 100m, go straight on through a gate on a Land Rover track sign-posted Shinagag farm.

After a further 1ml/1½km (NN 923679), leave the track beside a hut to climb Carn Liath, which now rises ahead as a giant cone.

A short stretch of boggy moor separates you from the foot of Carn Liath's south-west ridge, up which a wide, eroded path can be seen climbing to the summit. To avoid the worst of the bog, go left beside a fence for a couple of hundred metres, then right beside an old stone wall.

A path develops and, when the wall turns left at the 470m contour, keeps going up the ridge. It becomes steeper and stonier with height, but zigzags help to reduce the gradient and provide a fast-track to the ▲ summit.

The ascent path leaves the approach track beside a hut

CARN LIATH

Loch Moraig

The path up Carn Liath

Bonus Munros: BCCB & Carn nan Gabhar
add-on 7½ml/12km, 600m/1950ft

As can be seen from the map on Page 5, extending the route to Beinn a' Ghlo's two more distant Munros requires considerably more commitment. Beyond Carn Liath, a broad ridge sweeps onwards in fine style, snaking left, right then left again to cross a 760m/2500ft bealach and make a steep 310m/1000ft re-ascent to ▲Braigh Coire Chruinn-bhalgain (whose evocative Gaelic name is often understandably shortened to BCCB).

Beyond here the ridge twists right and left again over a small rise. A couple of hundred metres beyond the rise, at NN 952727, leave the ridge to descend a stony path on the right to the 847m/2780ft Bealach an Fhioda (*Byalach an Ee-igha*, Timber Pass) between BCCB and Carn nan Gabhar. The return route descends from the bealach, so anyone not wishing to climb 282m/926ft to the third, final and highest Munro can bail out here.

On the far side of the bealach, the path forks half-way up the hillside. The high road (right branch) gives the better going. It takes you onto the saddle between ΔAirgiod Bheinn (*Errakat Ven*, Silver Mountain) and Carn na Gabhar, and so onto the latter's bouldery summit ridge.

BCCB

CARN NAN GABHAR

Airgiod Bheinn

Bealach an Fhioda

return route

The quartzite rock ▲ summit is marked by the third of three large cairns, c.200m beyond the trig. point at the second. For dramatic views of Beinn a' Ghlo's craggiest scenery, wander a short distance further to peer over at remote Loch Loch, 680m/2230ft below.

To return to Loch Moraig, retrace steps to the Bealach an Fhioda and descend a path from there into the glen on the left (south-west). The path crosses the stream twice before leaving it to contour around the lower slopes of Carn Liath. You do not want to miss this contour path as it is the only sane way back through the heather. It is boggy to begin with but improves to become a good path back to the Shinagag track, which it joins near a track junction at NN 939682.

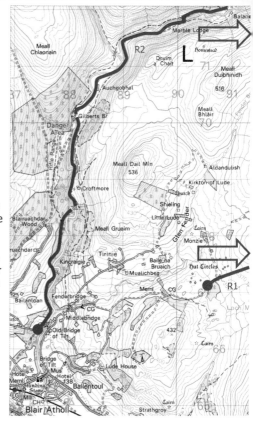

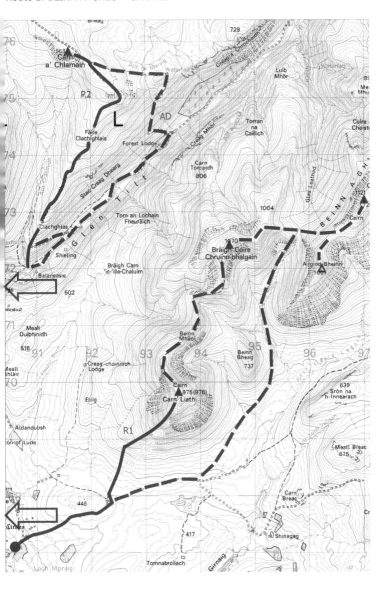

Carn a' Chlamain 192 963m/3159ft
(OS 43, NN 915758) more correctly Carn a' Chlamhain,
Carn a Chlahvin, Cairn of the Buzzard or Kite

CARN A'
CHLAMAIN

Viewed from Carn Liath of Beinn a' Ghlo

This remote hill top is the highest of several that face Beinn a' Ghlo across upper Glen Tilt. Hidden from the glen by steep, convex hillsides, its summit is distinguished from other nondescript moorland heights on the west side of the glen by a quartzite summit cone that drops a skirt of steep scree on its south side.

When it was permissible to drive the 7ml/11km up the glen to Forest Lodge, the stalkers' path from there to the summit made ascent easy. Since the closure of the road, it has become more normal to save a couple of miles by beginning near the old cottage of Balaneasie, a mere 5ml/8km up the glen. The good news, if that is how you choose to view it, is that the ascent from here has now been made even easier than from Forest Lodge, owing to the building of a Land Rover track up the gentle south-west ridge.

N.B. For information on access during the stalking season (August 1– October 20) visit www.outdooraccess-scotland.com/hftsh or phone Blair Atholl 01796-481-740.

The complete route, from car park to summit, will not endear itself to adrenaline junkies as it could just as easily be accomplished on four wheels as on foot. On the other hand, anyone who loves a good tramp will find here a route of zero difficulty, testing length and fine views along Glen Tilt.

In the good old days it was permissible to drive up Glen Tilt to Forest Lodge, which allowed ready access not only to Carn a' Chlamain and Beinn a' Ghlo but also to other Munros further upglen.

The road was closed on April Fool's Day 1996 (surely no coincidence?) on the recommendation of the (pre National Park) Cairngorm Working Party, whose members espoused the notion of 'the long walk-in'. We leave it to you to thank them or otherwise.

Carn a' Chlamain from Old Blair near Blair Atholl via Glen Tilt, Balaneasie and South-west Ridge

NN 875663, 16ml/26km, 810m/2650ft
Old Blair to Balaneasie return: 10ml/16km, outward ascent 120m/400ft
Balaneasie to Carn a' Chlamain return: 6ml/10km, 690m/2250ft

SW Ridge

Glen Tilt

CARN A' CHLAMAIN

From the car park at Old Bridge of Tilt, walk up the glen for 5ml/8km to the foot of the south-west ridge, opposite the old cottage at Balaneasie across the River Tilt. The foot of the ridge is squeezed between Glen Tilt to its right and a deep gorge full of waterfalls to its left, such that the lower slopes are quite steep. To avoid these, the Land Rover track up the ridge begins at Clachghlas, a further 900m up Glen Tilt, from where it climbs back to the ridge crest above the steep section.

For hillwalkers, a grassy path leaves the Glen Tilt track at the foot of the ridge to climb the right-hand side of the gorge and join the Land Rover track on the ridge crest. Alternatively, you can detour to Clachghlas to minimise the angle of ascent, following in the footsteps of Queen Victoria, but the path is an easy short cut.

Carn a' Chlamain was the first of several Munros climbed by Queen Victoria. At the age of 25, she ascended it by pony from Clachghlas in the autumn of 1844 (no stalking restrictions for QV). She found the summit view 'beautiful, nothing but mountains all around us, and the solitude, the complete solitude, very impressive'.

The map for this route is
combined with that for
Carn Liath on Pages 4 & 5.

CARN A' CHLAMAIN

The stony but
eminently hikeable track
goes all the way up the
broad, heathery ridge,
which is known as Faire
(*Fay-ra*) Clach-ghlais (the
Faire being the Skyline or
Guardian of Clachghlas,
itself meaning Grey Stone). Higher up,
the track considerably stays right of
the crest in order to avoid any cold
northerly wind that might be blowing.
Alternatively, sample the old path that
predates the track and still runs along
the crest.

Around the 770m contour the track
reaches a flattish saddle below steeper
slopes that rise to Chlamain's south-
east shoulder (known as Grianan Mor,
meaning Big Sunny Place). To
maintain a gentle angle, the track

detours right before climbing back left
onto the shoulder. You may prefer to
take a short cut on the old path, which
climbs more steeply, straight up the
shoulder, to rejoin the track on top.

The track bypasses Chlamain's
▲ summit on the north side, again
considerably leaving you a climb of
some 30m/100ft or so up quartzite
rubble to give you a greater feeling
of achievement. If you like wild
moorland, you may enjoy the view
as much as Queen Victoria did.

BEINN A' GHLO

alternative
descent
route

ascent
route

CARN A' CHLAMAIN

Alternative Descent: Forest Lodge add-on: 2ml/3km

To avoid retracing steps down the track, the old stalkers' path from Forest Lodge can be used as an alternative descent route to Glen Tilt. A few short sections can become boggy after rain, but in general its mostly stony surface is no worse than that of the track. It leaves you with an extra 2ml/3km walk back to the car park from Forest Lodge, but it gives good views up and down the glen as it zigzags down the steep hillside above the lodge.

On descent, the path forks left (east) from the ATV track at a bend on the shallow saddle between Grianan Mor and Chlamain's summit (NN 920756). The fork is more obvious aerially (i.e. when viewed from the summit) than it is on the ground, but cairns mark the way. The path crosses the plateau and plummets down the hillside above Glen Tilt. Despite the steep angle, it improves in quality as it descends, giving a knee-friendly descent on switchbacks as beautifully contoured as you would expect of a stalkers' path.

Nearing the wood above Forest Lodge, ignore a steeper branch that descends right into the trees and keep contouring left to a stile over a fence. The path descends beside the fence and around the trees to deposit you in Glen Tilt at the left-hand edge of the wood. Now for that 7ml/11km walk back down the glen. We could blether away about the beauty of the riverside walk, but we suspect your appreciation of it will diminish with distance.

The long road home

Glen Tilt

A must-see in the Blair Atholl area are the Falls of Bruar near the junction of the A9 and the B8079 (NN 818633). Made famous by Robert Burns' 1797 poem, these finest waterfalls in Perthshire consist of lower, middle and upper falls (20m/65ft high), with viewpoints and paths linked by two arched stone bridges.

▲ Carn na Caim 232 941m/3087ft (OS 42, NN 677821)
Carn na Ky-im, Peak of the Curve (i.e. its circular northern corrie)
▲ A' Bhuidheanach Bheag 240 936m/3071ft
(OS 42, NN 660776) *A Vooyanach Vake*, The Little Yellow Place

CARN NA CAIM   The East Drumochter Plateau

A9

Dalwhinnie

These two excessively flat-topped Munros flank the A9 just outside Dalwhinnie. As the average height of the East Drumochter Plateau on which they stand is c.850m/2800ft, it would be unfair to expect them to soar majestically above the roadside in classic pyramid fashion. On the other hand, the plateau gives a top-of-the-world walk to two easy summits that seem far more remote than their location beside the A9 would suggest.

Fortunately or unfortunately, depending on your view on such aesthetic matters, a Land Rover track climbs all the way onto the plateau, reaching a height of 900m/2950ft almost exactly equidistant between the two summits. Once up, the track forks to send branches both north and south towards each Munro.

Although upland vehicle tracks routinely outrage traditionalists, this particular one gives a speedy ascent away from the A9, enabling you to get 'away from it all' in minimal time.

In fact, if you promise not to tell anyone, we would go further. Although the two summits may win no awards for pulchritude, the ascent can, under sunny skies, give a very pleasant leg-stretch. So choose a good day, leave your preconceptions at the roadside and you may well find this extended stroll shamefully enjoyable.

Carn na Caim is the more straight-forward peak to reach, while those in search of an extended workout can double their Munro tally by climbing A' Bhuidheanach Bheag as well.

Carn na Caim from near Dalwhinnie (A9)
NN 640821, 7½ml/12km, 600m/1950ft

The Land Rover approach track begins on the A9 c.700m south of the Dalwhinnie turn-off. Park at the start (without blocking the gate) or at a lay-by 200m to the north. Well seen from the roadside, the track heads diagonally across the hillside before climbing more steeply up a shoulder between streams. It becomes stony higher up, but its surface is infinitely preferable to the surrounding moorland and a path beside it on the right alleviates any rough going.

The track climbs to an old quartz quarry at a height of 900m/2950ft, almost on the crest of the plateau. Older maps show it ending here, but

ATV tracks now continue across the plateau in each direction.

Just beyond the quarry's shale remnants, look for a left branch that heads north to Carn na Caim. This soon reaches the plateau crest and runs along it beside an old fence. After crossing a minor rise, it continues towards a higher rise seen ahead, which forms the summit.

The track doesn't go all the way, so leave it when it bears left across the hillside and keep going beside the fence, which carries straight on. A few hundred metres before the ▲ summit, the fence turns right. Leave it here and aim directly for the cairn ahead.

The track to the East Drumochter Plateau

A9

At the summit of Carn na Caim, it is worth walking a short distance beyond the cairn to the rim of its deep, circular northern corrie (Coire Cam, *Corra Caam*, Curving Corrie), which gives the mountain its name. You'll obtain good views of Meall Chuaich (R4) and Loch Cuaich across the corrie depths (picture on Page 15).

From the summit, it is tempting to take a direct route back to the roadside across the mouth of Coire Uilleim (*Corra Oolyam*, William's Corrie), but it doesn't save any time. The vegetation gets thicker as you descend, and traipsing across boggy moor isn't our idea of a fun end to the day. We'd recommend returning to the quarry and re-descending the approach track.

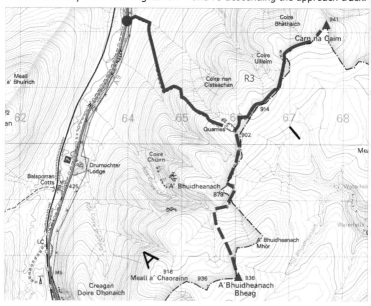

The track across the plateau to Carn na Caim

The final stretch (1)

CARN NA CAIM

Bonus Munro: A' Bhuidheanach Bheag
add-on 5ml/8km, 330m/1100ft

After retracing steps to the quarry, A' Bhuidheanach Bheag isn't *that* far away, but reaching it involves a convoluted route, pathless terrain and a stream crossing.

From the quarry, take the track that heads south across the plateau, in the opposite direction from Carn na Caim. It crosses a rise and reaches another rise named A' Bhuidheanach (NN 657791), quirkily 57m/188ft lower than its 'little' Munro sibling.

At the cairn on A' Bhuidheanach, look for an initially indistinct branch track that forks left at a right-angle. This soon improves to make the short descent to the peaty bealach below A'

Bhuidheanach Bheag. Follow the track to its end, at the stream that flows down from the bealach's far right-hand side (NN 655788).

Across the stream, a developing path beside a smaller stream climbs onto the continuing plateau. When the path becomes indistinct, keep going in the same direction to cross a brow and see the summit of the Munro ahead, marked by a trig. pillar on the highest point of the plateau. To avoid a section of peaty flats, trend left to reach an old fence that runs all the way up to the lonely ▲ summit. Then retrace steps to the quarry and descend to the roadside.

A' BHUIDHEANACH BHEAG

Spot the difference:
The final stretch (2)

▲ Meall Chuaich 214 951m/3120ft (OS 42, NN 716878)

Myowl Choo-ich, Quaich Hill, named for Loch Cuaich
(A quaich is a shallow two-handled Scottish drinking bowl)

MEALL CHUAICH

Cuaich
Aqueduct

Although this Munro to the north-west of Dalwhinnie looks little more than a big heathery lump on first viewing, its isolation gives it real presence compared to neighbouring Carn na Caim (R3), while Loch Cuaich at its foot makes an estimable attempt at picturesqueness.

The hydro track that services the dammed loch eases access and makes a scenic approach route, especially in spring. The ascent itself is rendered equally easy by a well-worn, if occasionally peaty, Munroists' path.

Panorama of the Northern Cairngorms from the summit of Meall Chuaich

The approach track to Meall Chuaich runs beside the Cuaich Aqueduct, which collects water from Loch Cuaich and the surrounding area, including underground from Loch an t-Seilich in the Gaick Pass further east.

Loch an t-Seilich was dammed in 1941 and Loch Cuaich in 1961. Generating electricity at various power stations along the way, the scheme carries the water to Loch Ericht and eventually to the Tummel hydro-electric power scheme.

Meall Chuaich from Cuaich (A9)
NN 655867, 8ml/13km, 600m/1950ft

The hydro access track begins at a height of 350m/150ft on the A9 opposite Cuaich cottages, just north of Dalwhinnie. Park at the start of the track or in the lay-by just south of it. Walk up the track to join another that runs beside the Cuaich Aqueduct to Cuaich Power Station (NN 674868).

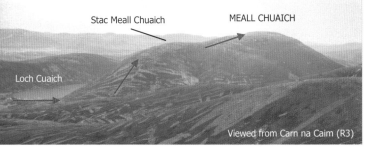

Stac Meall Chuaich   MEALL CHUAICH

Loch Cuaich

Viewed from Carn na Caim (R3)

Beyond the power station, a rougher track continues beside the Allt Cuaich to Loch Cuaich, situated in a trench beneath Meall Chuaich's steep western hillside. Keep left at a fork just beyond the power station, then left again at a stream further along (NN 681869) to reach the vicinity of the loch.

Stac Meall Chuaich   MEALL CHUAICH

Loch Cuaich

Allt Cuaich

Visiting Loch Cuaich (on the return trip?) requires only a short detour, but don't be tempted to descend directly to the loch via the corrie north of Stac Meall Chuaich. The hillside here is very steep and the ankle-grabbing heather is very atrocious.

Stac Meall Chuaich

Allt Coire Chuaich

At the network of tracks around the mouth of Loch Cuaich, keep to the one that bears right to climb into Coire Chuaich on the mountain's south side. The track passes a locked bothy and, a few hundred metres further along, bridges the Allt Coire Chuaich. On the first bend beyond the bridge, around a further 60m away, the ascent proper begins at last, 2½ml/4km from the roadside (NN 693869). An obvious boot-worn path leaves the track to take a *directissima* route up the hillside.

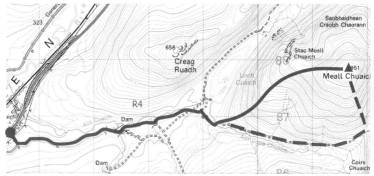

Worth a visit while in the area are the Falls of Truim, a few miles further up the A9 at NN 680922, where the River Truim showcases a series of 3-4m high woodland falls.

The path can be boggy at first but improves with height. If possible, go in a dry spell, when its eroded, knee-friendly sponginess makes it shamefully pleasurable, especially on descent. The path climbs steeply onto the mountain's west shoulder and, as the angle lessens with height, improves on grass and boulders.

The lower path: in spring frozen ground makes for firmer going

Thanks to a few crags on its north-west side, the domed shoulder revels in the fanciful name of Stac Meall Chuaich. The title Stac (*Stachk*, Stack) is normally reserved for rocky peaks.

Approaching the shoulder, the path veers right to become a stony highway up Meall Chuaich's broad, gentle west ridge. Smaller paths across the heath to each side ensure that the going remains good, although erosion here will eventually only increase the width of the stony central path. The skyline ahead is a false summit, but the true ▲ summit lies not far beyond, set in the middle of a flat plateau (what else, hereabouts?).

For variety there is an alternative route down, although it is neither as quick nor as easy. It descends the mountain's steep southern hillside of moss and heather beside fence posts, to reach the top of the track you quit earlier, on the bealach at the head of Coire Chuaich. A return this way will give you the mountain to yourself on a busy day, but it adds a steeper and rougher descent to a lengthier walk-out. (Avoid during the stalking season.)

Stac Meall Chuaich   MEALL CHUAICH

Traffic Scotland maintains real-time CCTV cameras facing both north and south along the A9 at Drumochter Pass, and these can be accessed to obtain current weather information. View live images at www.trafficscotland.org/lev/index.aspx.

▲ **The Cairnwell** 245 933m/3061ft (OS 43, NO 134773)
in Gaelic Carn Bhalg *(Carn Valak,* Cairn of the Bags, i.e. Peatbanks)
▲ **Carn a' Gheoidh** 180 975m/3199ft (OS 43, NO 107767)
Carn a Yawee, Goose Cairn
▲ **Carn Aosda** 278 917m/3009ft (OS 43, NO 134792)
Carn Ersta, Ancient Cairn

THE CAIRNWELL

Cairnwell
Pass

Glen Shee

Оn approach from the south along the A93, The Cairnwell soars above upper Glen Shee in classic pyramid style, promising a challenging ascent. The reality is somewhat different. Despite the peak's eminence when viewed from this angle, the A93 climbs to a height of 650m/2150ft at the Cairnwell Pass on its east side, and from there a chairlift takes tourists to within a few hundred metres of the summit. The misleading first impression is further punctured by the infrastructure of Scotland's largest ski area, whose unsightly tows bedeck each side of the Pass.

However, given such a high starting point, even without using the Cairnwell Chairlift, and with apologies to those who like their mountains remote and difficult, one can have few complaints about there being at least one Munro that allows itself to be bagged in a few hours. And if such a short day proves insufficient exercise, neighbouring Munros Carn Aosda and Carn a' Gheoidh can be added to the trip to triple your Munro tally.

The Cairnwell Pass mountains look their best in winter, when snow blankets ground churned up and worn bare by the demands of a snowsports centre. The Cairnwell makes a fine winter viewpoint easily reached from the top of the chairlift (with appropriate winter gear for a summit track that may be snowbound or icy). At such times, try to ignore downhill sliders who blemish the foreground, and remember to wear dark glasses to combat the visual pollution of ski and snowboard attire.

The Cairnwell from the Cairnwell Pass (A93)
NO 138781, 2½ml/4km, 280m/900ft

The Cairnwell rises directly above the Cairnwell Pass, giving it the (dubious?) honour of sporting the shortest ascent route of any Munro. Nevertheless, the terrain is occasionally steep and pathless, so pace yourself and be prepared for a short, sharp aerobic workout.

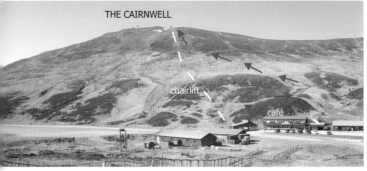

THE CAIRNWELL

chairlift

café

Start up the rough track that begins on the right of the chairlift beside the café (open all year round). The track curves away right then veers back left towards the chairlift pylons, becoming even rougher. When it turns sharp right again to cross the hillside, take the indistinct path that carries straight on. This climbs steeply to the right of a broken ski fence before cutting left to climb beside the pylons. Take comfort in the knowledge that it is not as far to the chairlift's upper station as it looks.

Once there, only a few hundred metres of rough track separate you from The Cairnwell's ▲ summit, whose unsightly radio masts resolutely detract from communion with Nature.

For a less steep descent, retrace steps to the top of the chairlift then keep going down the track, which runs along the skyline all the way to Carn Aosda. It crosses a rise and descends to a low point between the two Munros, from where another track branches right to give an effortless descent to the café. If you are deterred by the steepness of the ascent route described, this track makes a very easy alternative way up.

The skyline track   CARN AOSDA

THE CAIRNWELL

Descent options

Bonus Munros:
Carn Aosda alone add-on ½ml/1km, 120m/400ft
Carn a' Gheoidh and Carn Aosda add-on 4ml/7km, 290m/950ft

The track that runs along the skyline from The Cairnwell goes all the way to Carn Aosda. Beyond its low point, the summit of this second Munro is only 122m/401ft higher and should think itself lucky to find itself in Munro's Tables at all. To reach it, simply follow the track all the way to its end at the top of the Carn Aosda T-bar, at which point you have just walked past the ▲ summit cairn atop the rockpile on the left.

At the low point on the track that connects The Cairnwell to Carn Aosda, Loch Vrotachan lies barely 50m/160ft below.

On a sunny day its inviting shoreline makes an idyllic picnic spot, easily reached for a modicum of extra effort.

From the summit, retrace steps a few hundred metres to the top of parallel ski fences, on the right-hand side of which another track gives a swift descent to the café.

To extend a very short day, you can bag a third Munro before descending by making a return trip to Carn a' Gheoidh, although this requires a tad more effort. If you decide to go for it, do so *before* heading for Carn Aosda as it lies west of The Cairnwell.

Descending from The Cairnwell, the track crosses a rise. Leave it here for a path that branches left around the rim of Coire Dirich (*Corra Jeerich*, Ascending Corrie) to the low point at the corrie head.

Beyond here, the path passes a couple of attractive ridge-top lochans and undulates up to the rounded rise of Carn nan Sac. It contours right of the highest point and crosses the broad, plateau-like ridge of heath and turf beyond to climb to Carn a' Gheoidh's stony ▲ summit dome.

Retrace steps to the dip at the head of Coire Dirich then keep left on a contouring path that regains the skyline track just above the 795m/2609ft low point between The Cairnwell and Carn Aosda.

Descent from Carn Aosda   THE CAIRNWELL

▲Glas Tulaichean 79 1051/3448ft (OS 43, NO 051760)
Glass Toolichan, Green Knolls

GLAS TULAICHEAN

Glas Choire Mhor

Gleann Taitneach

Viewed from
the east

Well away from the Glenshee ski slopes, Glas Tulaichean lies at the apex of a number of gentle green ridges, two of which enclose the huge Glas Choire Mhor (*Glass Chorra Voar*, Big Green Corrie). From Dalmunzie (*Dalmoonie*), near the Spittal of Glenshee on the A93, an ATV track goes all the way to the summit.

We leave you to decide whether the track is A Good Thing or A Bad Thing, but at least it makes the ascent a doddle. Interestingly, despite such a man-made intrusion into the landscape, the remote country to the west, around the upper reaches of Glen Tilt, adds a surprising sense of wildness to the ambience of the ascent.

For a bit more effort, Alternative Descents 1 & 2 vary the return route.

After the storm: summit
view over Loch nan Eun

Glas Tulaichean South Ridge from Dalmunzie (near Spittal of Glenshee, A93)

NO 091712, 10ml/16km, 690m/2250ft

Begin at Dalmunzie Hotel, at the end of the private road from the Spittal of Glenshee (small parking fee payable at reception). If the access policy changes, you'll have to park at the end of the public road at NO 105702 and add an each-way 1ml/1½km road walk to the day.

Glenlochsie Lodge (ruin)

Former light railway track

From the hotel, follow the paved road to Glenlochsie Farm then turn left between farm buildings to find the start of the Land Rover track that continues up Glen Lochsie. When the track crosses the Glen Lochsie Burn (eventually to re-cross it further along), avoid the double ford by staying on the near side of the river.

Just before the first crossing point, take the grassy track that doubles back to zigzag up the hillside and traverse gently up the glen to the ruins of Glenlochsie Lodge.

The lodge stands on the far side of the Allt Clais Mhor (*Owlt Clash Voar*, Stream of the Big Trench), at its junction with the Glen Lochsie Burn.

GLAS TULAICHEAN

The track lower down

Cross the stream (on stepping stones) to rejoin the Land Rover track and follow it up Tulaichean's long, broad, curving south ridge. It climbs steeply at first, then eases off before steepening again to the summit, seen ahead as the highest of the eponymous Green Knolls.

The grassy Glen Lochsie track is the bed of a unique former light railway line that was built to convey Victorian sportsmen (i.e. deer stalkers) up to the lodge. The track from there to Glas Tulaichean's summit makes the ascent straightforward. Now if only some enlightened philanthropist would re-open that railway…

At the track's high-point, just before it bears left down Tulaichean's west ridge, you are only a few metres from the ▲summit. A rougher ATV track branches right to take you all the way to the cairn above the broken crags of Glas Choire Mhor's headwall.

The track higher up, looking back

Although the view over the corrie rim grabs the attention, the pure of heart will be equally seduced by the panorama to the west and north, where remote Munros dot wild country and the Northern Cairngorms are strung out like a frieze on the horizon.

Return the same way or, if you're feeling adventurous, vary the descent by choosing one of two alternative ways down.

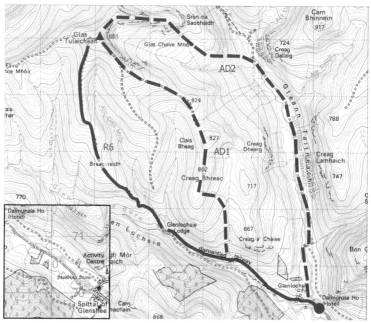

Alternative Descent 1: South-east Ridge

This alternative descent route, pathless lower down, descends Tulaichean's south-east ridge around the south rim of Glas Choire Mhor, giving views into the corrie and across Gleann Taitneach.

The ATV track at the summit takes you all the way down the heathy ridge to Point 827 at NO 071742. To find the easiest way down from here, continue south along the ridge over Creag Bhreac (*Craik Vrechk*, Speckled Crag), then bear left to descend beside the small stream that begins at NO 069733. All the hillsides hereabouts are beset by clinging heather, but stay close to the stream and you'll find game paths and grassy banks that make light of the descent. Rejoin the approach track to Glenlochsie Lodge at the point where it bridges the stream (NO 075721).

On Glas Tulaichean's south-east ridge in winter

Glas Choire Mhor

Alternative Descent 2: East Ridge

This alternative way down gives a return route of contrasting character that shows Glas Tulaichean at its best. It descends the mountain's most scenic ridge and returns to Dalmunzie along the great green glaciated trench that is Gleann Taitneach. It crosses steeper, boggier ground, is quite narrow at one point and requires stream crossings and more attention to routefinding.

The ridge in question is Tulaichean's east ridge, which forms the north rim of Glas Choire Mhor. From the summit, follow an indistinct path around the rim to the junction of the east ridge and the north-east ridge, then keep going around the rim. The grassy ridge is fairly narrow for a while and descends in a fine situation between

The record for the Glas Tulaichean hill race, from Dalmunzie Lodge to the summit, stands at just over half an hour. This is not a misprint.

GLAS TULAICHEAN

AD1

Glas Choire Mhor

AD2

Gleann Taitneach

the depths of Glas Choire Mhor and Glas Choire Bheag (*Vake*, Little), beyond which there are fine views across Loch nan Eun (*Yain*, Birds) to the Northern Cairngorms.

When the ridge broadens below a steepening, leave it to avoid craggy ground further down and descend right into the boggy bowl of Glas Choire Mhor. Continue down the grassy hillside below the corrie mouth into Gleann Taitneach, using any ATV tracks you have the luck to find.

Cross the Allt Ghlinn Taitneach to join the Land Rover track that runs down the glen. This river and a couple more further down (the Allt Aulich at NO 085748 and the Allt Coire Shith at NO 090724) are normally passable on stepping stones but will require fords when in spate.

Using the bridge at NO 089724, leave the track to re-cross the Allt Ghlinn Taitneach and follow a grassy path along the far bank back to Dalmunzie.

On Glas Tulaichean's east ridge in winter

NORTHERN CAIRNGORMS

Loch nan Eun

▲ Carn Bhac 221 946m/3104ft (OS 43, NO 051832)
Carn Vachk, Cairn of Peatbanks

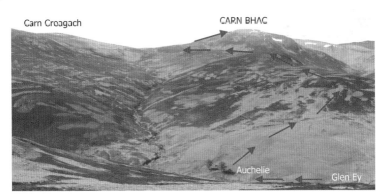

Carn Creagach   CARN BHAC

Auchelie   Glen Ey

Carn Bhac is the highest point on the peaty moors above Glen Ey west of Braemar. It is a retiring hill top whose ascent is often combined with that of neighbouring Munro Beinn Iutharn Mhor to make a long day, but the connection varies from steep and rocky to frustratingly boggy and is an unpleasant proposition.

Geomorphologically speaking, Carn Bhac suffers from being in the shadow of its higher and more sculpted neighbour. From some angles its summit is even difficult to distinguish from the surrounding moors.

However, while some mountains flatter to deceive, Carn Bhac hides in its recesses some noteworthy scenery, to which it grants easy access via two separate upland vehicle tracks that form the route described here. Such is the battle in the Cairngorms between those who wish to build such tracks and those who wish to erase them that maps have difficulty keeping up with the current situation. Hence these two tracks appear only on recent maps.

Our view? Even if you are no lover of vehicle tracks, only a militant environmental Luddite could begrudge them on this kind of terrain. What do you think?

One track climbs above picturesque Glen Ey while the other penetrates the lost valley of the Allt Connie. Rough ground can't be avoided altogether but, in combination, the two tracks turn an otherwise abysmal bogtrot into an unexpectedly rewarding round trip, with much to see along the way.

Carn Bhac boasts a tremendous panorama of the Northern Cairngorms beyond the flatlands of Deeside. The high peaks seem surprisingly close at hand, with the reclusive Devil's Point (R17) especially prominent in slanting evening light.

Carn Bhac from Inverey near Braemar
NO 089892, 10½ml/17km, 620m/2050ft

Begin in Inverey, 5ml/8km west of Braemar. From the car park, 230m before the Ey Burn bridge, take the Land Rover track that runs up Glen Ey (*Eye*). The name derives from the Gaelic for God, hence God's Glen.

The Colonel's Bed   Auchelie

Lower Glen Ey

The track runs beside fields to the confluence of the Ey Burn and the Allt Connie (*Owlt Coney*, Firewood Stream), then it bridges the Ey Burn and makes a brief climb to contour across the hillside high above the river. After c.1½ml/2km, on a sharp right-hand bend, look below left for an obvious path to the Colonel's Bed (see below). The path rejoins the track further along and is worth the detour.

After 2ml/3km the track reaches the ruins of Auchelie farm. Leave it here for a side track that climbs the grassy hillside behind onto the gentle north ridge of Carn Creagach (*Carn Craikach*, Craggy Cairn), the moorland rise just east of Carn Bhac. The hillside becomes increasingly heathery but this only makes the track more welcome.

CARN BHAC

The track through the heather

The Colonel's Bed (NO 087871) lies in the picturesque linn (gorge) of the Ey Burn. It was here, in a rocky recess, that John Farquharson of Inverey, called the 'Black Colonel' on account of his dark appearance, hid from the redcoats after defeat at the Battle of Killiecrankie in 1689. A recent landslip has impeded access to the site but the finest part of the linn in any case lies further up, where the river funnels down a series of small waterfalls. Take care at the cliff edge.

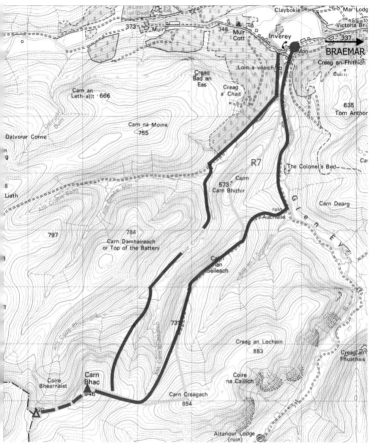

As the broad ridge levels out above the deep glen of the Allt Connie on the right, the track gives dream going across terrain that would otherwise be the stuff of nightmares. Carn Bhac did not get its Gaelic name for nothing.

As if to underscore the benefits of upland vehicle tracks, this one ends at 710m/2350ft on the last dip in the

ridge below Carn Creagach, leaving you a taster of what progress would be like in its absence. Prepare for a spot of marshy tramping.

Ahead lies the rounded hump of Carn Creagach. To its right, across a bealach at the head of the Allt Connie, lies the giant pimple of Carn Bhac. Take a moment to study its facing north-east spur, which forms the descent route.

CARN BHAC

Steepening

NE Spur

To avoid crossing Carn Creagach and spending more time than necessary on the marshy moorland, tramp straight across the hillside from the end of the track to the bealach. Above here, slopes of heath give better going up to the quartzite-strewn flat roof of Carn Bhac's ▲ summit.

From here, you could return to Inverey by the route of ascent but, for a slightly steeper, off-track descent, a return by the north-east spur and the glen of the Allt Connie makes a satisfying round trip. It's also a slightly shorter way back.

Well seen on ascent, the north-east spur descends directly to the glen, with a steep section of awkward heather and quartzite not far below the summit. This steepening can be turned on its immediate right but it is easier to give it a wider berth. Walk back down towards the Carn Creagach bealach for a few hundred metres then curve down around the foot of the steepening on gentle grass slopes to gain the spur at a boggy levelling.

The going here isn't great for a while, but you can't avoid rough terrain entirely on *any* route on Carn Bhac. Beyond the levelling, keep left to find easier grass slopes that descend

to the Allt Coire Bhearnaist (*Vyarnist*, Gap) just above its confluence with the Allt Connie.

On the far bank of the Allt Connie, look for the low ruins of a shieling at NO 061848. This heralds the start of an easy walk back to Inverey along a path that soon becomes a grassy ATV track. Don't worry if you don't find the shieling as you'll soon find the track beside the river. It leads all the way down to the Allt Connie's confluence with the Allt Christie Mor (from Gaelic *Criosda*, meaning Big Swift Stream).

Just before the confluence, the mouth of the glen of the Allt Connie appears to be blocked by the steep hillside of Carn Bhithir (*Bi-hir*, Serpent, Demon or Thunderbolt). This *trompe l'oeil* effect gives the worrying impression that you are heading *into* rather than out of the mountains. It is a strange phenomenon that gives the otherwise featureless glen the feel of a true 'lost valley', across whose grassy flats the track makes effortless

---

Top baggers in need of further exercise at the summit will find a short return trip along the south-west ridge an attractive high-level stroll. Cross a shallow saddle to the ΔSouth-west Top and a second shallow saddle to the former Top of Carn a' Bhutha. The terrain is surprisingly excellent and the ridge affords rare views of the northern reaches of Beinn a' Ghlo (R1).
Return trip: 3ml/5km, 120m/400ft.

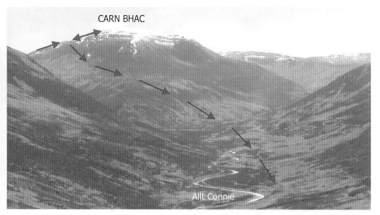

CARN BHAC

Allt Connie

progress. Look out for other ruined shielings from a bygone age.

The track bridges the Allt Christie Mor and joins a Land Rover track that descends through woods on the left (west) bank of the continuing Allt Connie to its junction with the Ey Burn. Just before the confluence, some fine rapids and waterfalls may well lure you into taking a closer look. The track continues along the left bank of the Ey Burn to reach the roadside just west of the car park at Inverey. N.B. The former bridge at NO 086884, which gave access to the east-side track on which you began the day, no longer exists.

Waterfall on the Allt Connie

If you're in Braemar with time on your hands, three short walks lead to hill tops whose views of the Northern Cairngorms rival those from Carn Bhac. **Morrone** (NO 132886, 859m/2819ft) can be reached by a vehicle track from Glen Clunie, south of Braemar, or more pleasantly by an excellent path from the car park at the head of Chapel Brae in Braemar (NO 143911, 4ml/6km, 490m/1600ft).

Carn Mor (NO 103872, 706m/2317ft) can be reached by another excellent track that climbs almost to the summit from Inverey (NO 089892, 4ml/6km, 360m/1200ft). From the top of Hillside Road in Braemar yet another excellent path climbs the lower **Creag Choinnich** (NO 161918, 538m/1766ft) for views up and down the Dee Valley and of the Eastern Cairngorms (NO 154913, 1ml/1½km, 200m/5650ft).

▲ **Glas Maol** 69 1068m/3504ft (OS 43, NO 167765)
Glas Meul, Bald Green Hill
▲ **Cairn of Claise** 71 1064m/3491ft (OS 43, NO 185788)
Cairn of Clasha, Cairn of the Furrow or Trench

Cairnwell Pass

R8

GLAS MAOL

Ｎorth and east of the Cairnwell Pass, the A93 curves down into Deeside around the foot of a great rolling tableland whose height enables no less than 14 highpoints to achieve Munro status. The area is known as the White Mounth (from the Gaelic *Monadh*, meaning Moor).

The Munros pepper sky-touching country characterised by easy terrain and seemingly limitless horizons, where there is always one more Munro or Top to climb. If you love to go a-wanderin' with your knapsack on your back, this is the place to do it.

The most westerly Munro is Glas Maol, which dominates the east side of the Cairnwell Pass as effectively as The Cairnwell (R5) dominates the west side. Viewed from the road, its summit is hidden behind a ski-tow-bedecked north-west shoulder (Meall Odhar), above which its vast, domed summit radiates ridges in all directions.

THE CAIRNWELL

Owing to its central position in the ski area, the ascent is no walk on the wild side, but Glas Maol is such a substantial mountain that the short ascent will take you out of sight and sound of the ironmongery to give you a taste of the White Mounth's wide horizons.

Glas Maol from the Cairnwell Pass (A93)
NO 141775, 4ml/6km, 430m/1400ft

From the south end of the huge Cairnwell Pass car park, a rough ski access track climbs 260m/850ft straight up the hillside beside ski fencing to ΔMeall Odhar (*Myowl Oa-er*, Dun-coloured Hill). The track is steep in places and allows no warm-up approach, so don't be lured by its brevity into rushing it (or envying skiers who get towed up in winter).

Over the top of Meall Odhar, on more pleasant going, a path continues across a shallow dip. It then climbs in tight zigzags up a steep slope beside a small corrie, whose rim often carries a wreath of snow until late spring. You emerge onto Glas Maol's pancake-flat summit plateau, which impresses by its sheer size. The ▲ summit is at the far end.

The path beyond Meall Odhar   GLAS MAOL

Curiously, the minor excrescence of Meall Odhar has succeeded in holding on to Top status through every revision of Munro's Tables since 1891, despite the fact that it rises only c.10m above its surroundings. Surely bribery must have been involved.

Glas Maol summit plateau   Summit

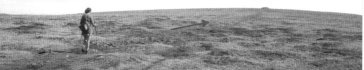

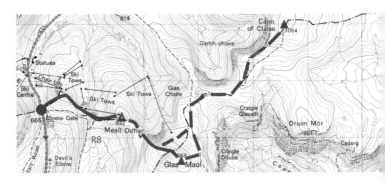

Bonus Munro: **Cairn of Claise** add-on 4ml/6km, 230m/750ft

A t the summit of Glas Maol, other Munros lie to north and south. To the south, Creag Leacach (*Craik Lyech -kach*, Slabby Crag) lies only 2ml/3km away, but it is a big rockpile whose negotiation crosses awkward, bouldery terrain and steep slopes beyond. If you wish to extend the day by bagging a second Munro, a more congenial option is Cairn of Claise, which lies barely further away to the north.

From Glas Maol, descend easy slopes in a north-east direction to reach a vehicle track that crosses the flanks of the mountain less than 50m/

150ft below. Turn left to follow the track around a bend and across the tableland to Cairn of Claise between deep corries to left and right.

After passing a low point, the track aims right of Cairn of Claise's rounded summit. Leave it to stay on the high ground to the left as the plateau narrows to form Cairn of Claise's south-west ridge. A wall runs along the crest and traces of a path beside it soon propel you to the ▲summit.

On return to Glas Maol, you can bypass the summit itself by taking a shortcut across the slopes to its north.

CAIRN OF CLAISE

▲ Tolmount 202 958m/3143ft (OS 44, NO 210800)

Mountain of the Dale (i.e. Glen Doll), originally the name of the drove road (now called Jock's Road) that passes close to its summit

▲ Tom Buidhe 204 957m/3140ft (OS 43, NO 213787)

Towm Boo-ya, Yellow Hill

TOLMOUNT

Viewed from the north
(R9 approaches from
the south)

Loch Callater

These two dumpy hill tops are set in the heart of wild country east of Glen Shee. Far from any roadside, they would be very awkward to reach were it not for Jock's Road, which crosses close to Tolmount's summit.

The mountain itself lacks notable features, but the scenery along Jock's Road is constantly interesting and more than compensates. Tom Buidhe's summit lies close by and can be added for little extra effort.

Jock's Road, formerly known as The Tolmounth, is an ancient route (now a path) that crosses the Mounth from Glen Clunie to Glen Clova. It was used by cattle drovers, thieves, smugglers and others.

Nineteenth century estate owners tried to ban its use but the Scottish Rights of Way Society opposed them. In a courtroom battle that went all the way to the House of Lords and left the society bankrupt, access was finally established in 1888.

Fifty-seven shepherds were called to give evidence. John Winter, for whom

Jock's Road is named, is often incorrectly reported as being one of them. In fact he lived a century earlier and was involved in a previous dispute that resulted in his flock of sheep being trapped for months on the high ground.

There has been a shelter at NO 233778 for centuries. Originally known as the Shieling of Lunkard, then Jock's Hut, it was rebuilt in 1966 by Davy Glen in memory of five walkers who perished in a blizzard on New Year's Day 1959. It is now known as Davy's Bourach (Gaelic for a shambles).

Tolmount from Glen Clova via Jock's Road
NO 284762, 12ml/19km, 770m/2500ft

Jock's Road: looking down Glen Doll

Glen Clova is the finest example in Scotland of a U-shaped valley slung between hanging corries, their lower halves sliced away by the glacier that scoured the trench. The route begins at the car park at the end of the road up the glen (small parking fee, 24hr toilet). Beside the car park is Glen Doll Ranger Base, where you can obtain leaflets and information. Further details: www.angus.gov.uk/leisure/rangerservice/angusglens.htm.

TOM BUIDHE

TOLMOUNT

Davy's Bourach

Jock's Road: looking up Glen Doll
from the Shank of Drumfollow (R10)

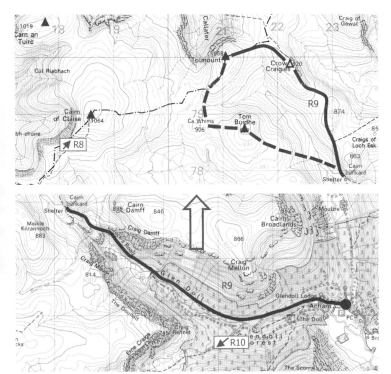

A forest track (Jock's Road) continues along Glen Doll (*Dole*, Dale), which Sir Hugh himself considered to be 'as wild a little glen as one could wish to see'. When the track bears left to cross the White Water at NO 268760 (R10), branch right on the forest path, signposted Jock's Road, that continues up the glen.

Once out of the forest, with the glen narrowing between sky-high crags, a path, renovated in 2006, climbs to a viewpoint and shelter at the glen head (NO 233778). At the time of writing, path renovation ends soon afterwards,

leaving rough going for a while as Jock's Road continues its climb around the slopes of Cairn Lunkard.

The going improves again as the path undulates along a broad ridge, passing Loch Esk in a peaty hollow below right, and reaching ΔCrow Craigies (Crow Craglets), Tolmount's subsidiary Top. Leave the path here to bear left across a shallow saddle and climb easy slopes of grass and heath to ▲Tolmount's nearby summit. Walk a short distance beyond the cairn to obtain views over Loch Callater to the Northern Cairngorms.

NORTHERN CAIRNGORMS

Loch Callater

The view from Tolmount

Bonus Munro: Tom Buidhe add-on zero mileage, 90m/300ft

TOLMOUNT

TOM BUIDHE

CAIRN OF CLAISE (R8)

Pudding-shaped Tom Buidhe lies only a short distance south of Tolmount, such that returning to Jock's Road via the summit adds no length and little ascent to the trip (although the terrain is pathless and boggier).

From Tolmount, a path descends grassy slopes to a pocket of boggy ground between the two Munros at around the 870m contour, then a brief ascent brings you to a connecting path from nearby Cairn of Claise (R8). This soon puts you at Tom Buidhe's ▲ summit.

TOM BUIDHE

TOLMOUNT

The rough upper reaches of Jock's Road

To regain Jock's Road, descend Tom Buidhe's grassy south-east slopes and cross a stretch of peaty ground to reach the path a few hundred metres above the shelter. **Tip**: Recce the best line down on the way up.

▲ Mayar 253 928m/3045ft (OS 44, NO 240737)

May-ar, possibly High Plain (from Gaelic *Magh + Ard*) or from *Maor* (formerly a king's official), referring to the peak's prominent position

▲ Driesh 219 947m/3107ft (OS 44, NO 271735)

Dreesh, meaning obscure; usually translated as Place of Brambles from Gaelic *Dris*, but this is unlikely

MAYAR

The path between Mayar and Driesh

The five Angus glens (Isla, Prosen, Clova, Lethnot and Esk) reach into the mountains north of Dundee like giant fingers. Since 2003 there has been an Angus Glens Walking Festival. For further details visit www.angusahead.com/walkingfestival.

These two plateau highpoints supply compelling evidence for the proposition that, however plain a summit may be, the ascent to it can still provide an outstanding day on the hill. On a round trip from Glen Clova, approach paths are excellent, the tableland of the White Mounth is a joy to saunter across and there is plenty of diverting corrie and waterfall scenery to view along the way.

Although the lower of the two Munros, Mayar harbours one of the most beautiful corries in the Highlands, through which the ascent path passes. An alternative descent route makes for a fine round trip, with the summit of nearby Driesh an optional extra.

Corrie Fee makes an excellent objective for a stroll between refreshments at Glen Clova Hotel or in Kirriemuir. Pick up a leaflet at Glen Doll Ranger Base beside the car park (see Page 36 for details).

Another popular excursion is to the perfect hanging corrie that holds Loch Brandy, 400m/1300ft up the hillside behind Glen Clova Hotel (NO 327731). Sadly, the loch contains only water.

Mayar from Glen Clova
NO 284761, 7ml/11km, 690m/2250ft

The route begins as for Route 9. Park in the car park at the end of the road up Glen Clova and take the forest track (Jock's Road) along Glen Doll (see Page 36 for full details). When Jock's Road branches right as a path at NO 268760, stay left on the main track, which bridges the White Water (NO 266758) and climbs through the forest to become an excellent path into Corrie Fee.

At the mouth of the corrie, barely an hour from the car park, the path exits the forest to reveal a magical hidden amphitheatre – a Shangri-La of meadow, stream and crag whose rare arctic and alpine flora are protected as a nature reserve.

The path winds its way around the glacial moraines that dot the corrie floor and climbs out the back, well to the left of a picturesque waterfall. Path improvements in the 2000s have made the steep ascent much easier than it used to be, while waterfall and corrie views provide constant diversion.

You emerge into a shallow basin that rises gradually onto the plateau above, which forms part of the White Mounth. The path runs across grass and heath and has a few boggy patches after rain. Without incident it

Coire Fee

In spring the hillsides are carpeted with anemones and violets.

Formerly part of Caenlochan National Nature Reserve, Corrie Fee (Deer Corrie) became an NNR itself in 2005. For detailed information on its history, flora and fauna, visit www.snh.org.uk/pdfs/publications/nnr/Corrie_Fee_NNR_Story.pdf.

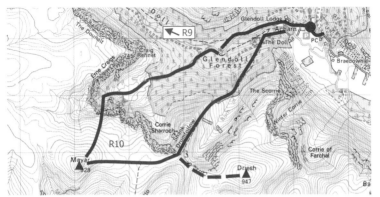

climbs gently upwards, revealing ever-expanding horizons, to the scattered rocks at Mayar's ▲summit.

The descent route makes use of an historic path to find a different way back with a whole new set of views. From Mayar, head east across the plateau towards Driesh. An initially indistinct path soon becomes a highway that is a pleasure to walk. At the top of the Shank of Drumfollow (the eastern rim of Corrie Fee) it is crossed by the Kilbo path, which links Glen Prosen (right) to Glen Clova (left).

Go left to follow the path down below the crest of the Shank into the forest. The stony upper section makes for poor going, but the lower section is pleasantly grassy. Some prefer to descend the grassy crest of the Shank itself, which carries a small path that joins the Kilbo Path near the forest fence. This way you'll obtain wonderful views over Corrie Fee and Jock's Road (picture on Page 36).

Once into the trees, the Kilbo Path descends to a forest track. Go straight across to short-cut a long bend and rejoin the track lower down at a hairpin bend. The track bridges the White Water at NO 276763 to rejoin Jock's Road not far from the car park.

DRIESH

Shank of Drumfollow

Viewed from Mayar

Shank of Drumfollow

Kilbo Path

Bealach

Viewed from Little Driesh

Bonus Munro: Driesh add-on 2ml/3km, 160m/550ft

From the top of the Shank of Drumfollow, only a shallow bealach separates you from the summit of Driesh, which looms sharply overhead. It's not far to the summit, but it's a stiff little climb.

Take one of the paths that branch right from the Shank to make the short descent to the 809m/2655ft bealach, then head skywards. The path climbs steeply up broken ground before easing off to contour around Driesh's west top (Little Driesh) to the ▲ summit dome. The summit trig. pillar and welcome stone windbreak lie 100m beyond the first cairn reached.

To descend, return to the Shank and regain the Kilbo path.

DRIESH

Little Driesh

Bealach

These Munros were well known to Sir Hugh Munro himself because they were the closest to his home at Lindertis, west of Kirriemuir. He calculated he could walk in a straight line across the White Mounth for ten miles and only once dip below 3000ft.

▲ **Broad Cairn** 142 998m/3275ft (OS 44, NO 240815)
possibly from Gaelic *Braighaid*, meaning Upland
▲ **Cairn Bannoch** 117 1012m/3321ft (OS 44,
NO 222825) possibly from Gaelic *Beannach*, meaning Peaked Cairn

South of Ballater on Deeside, Glen Muick carries a minor road that curves around the back of Lochnagar (R14) to give easy access to both that mountain and Broad Cairn, the two sturdy Munros at the head of the glen.

Beyond the road end at the Spittal of Glenmuick, the glen continues as a glacial trench that separates the two peaks and cradles two superb lochs. With a length of 2ml/3½km, picturesque Loch Muick is the largest body of water in the Cairngorms, while the secretive Dubh Loch (*Doo Loch*, Black Loch) is a beautiful mountain sanctuary sandwiched between immense crags – as imposing a spot as spots come in the Highlands.

The ascent of Broad Cairn, the highpoint above the Dubh Loch's southside crags, is both scenic and straightforward. A track along the shoreline of Loch Muick climbs onto the gentle east ridge and a path continues to the rocky summit.

On the drive back down Glen Muick, especially in wet weather, it's worth a roadside stop to view the two-tiered 10m/35ft waterfall at the Linn of Muick (NO 332895).

Broad Cairn from Glen Muick near Ballater
NO 310851, 12ml/19km, 630m/2100ft

From the Spittal of Glenmuick car park, take the track that carries straight on past the visitor centre and other buildings. Keep right at a fork after a few hundred metres (NO 304846) to reach Loch Muick and follow the track along its south-west shore. Half-way along, at the bridge over the Black Burn, the Diagonal Path branches right to continue along the lochside, climb Coire Chash (Steep Corrie) and rejoin the track higher up.

Although this renovated path is in excellent condition, a more scenic option is to stay on the track, which runs up to and along the edge of the plateau above the loch. For its zigzagging course, it is affectionately known as the Streak of Lightning (N.B. the name is often misleadingly applied to the Diagonal Path).

Once onto the plateau, the track makes a short 30m/100ft descent to end on a 700m/2300ft saddle, where an old pony hut (aka Allan's Hut; NO 256808) offers rudimentary shelter. The Diagonal Path rejoins the track 150m before the hut.

Paths now branch left and right. The left branch comes up from Glen Clova, while the route to Broad Cairn branches right to make the final 300m/1000ft ascent. The track used to go higher than the pony hut but it has been rewilded, leaving a deteriorating path that becomes increasingly indistinct. After topping a rise, several variations attempt to find the best line up steepening slopes of tiresome boulders to the ▲ summit.

The most scenic return route descends via the Dubh Loch, but it crosses steep, rough ground (see Alternative Descent). If you decide to return by the ascent route, you can still vary the descent by branching left down the Diagonal Path 150m beyond the pony hut. From the path foot you can then return along either side of Loch Muick.

Climbing the Streak of Lightning

Loch Muick

Just beyond the Spittal car park (small parking fee), there are toilets and a small visitor centre offering daytime refreshments and a 24hr drinks vending machine. Further info: email info@balmoralcastle.com.

The Spittal is named for a hospice or hospital, later an inn, that catered to travellers crossing the White Mount.

The 'Wandering Gowals' (see next page) have led a peripatetic Tables existence over the years. Craig of Gowal is mapped correctly on OS 44 and is listed correctly in the 1997 Tables. In 1981, however, it was mistakenly moved to Cairn of Gowal's true location (NO 226820; Point 991 on OS 44). This did not cause a clash because, until 1997, Cairn of Gowal was incorrectly listed in the Tables as Point 983 (NO 228816), where it still appears on the map.

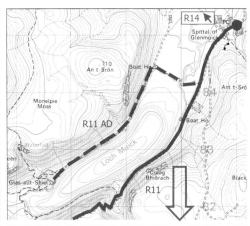

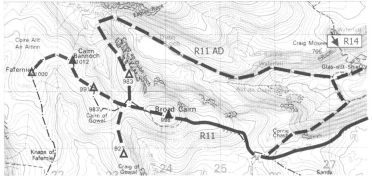

The view back down the ascent route from near the summit of Broad Cairn

Bonus Munro: Cairn Bannoch add-on 2½ml/4km, 220m/700ft

Beyond Broad Cairn, the rolling White Mounth bristles with Munros and Tops. For a taste of the possibilities here, take a return trip to Cairn Bannoch, the nearest Munro.

Over the top of Broad Cairn, boulders give way to gentle heath with excellent going, and a path soon reappears to descend 60m/200ft to a broad saddle. The gentle grassy slope on the right here rises to Creag an Dubh-loch and is used by the Alternative Descent.

Across the saddle, the path bears right to bypass Point 983 and climb 50m/160ft over flat-topped ΔCairn of Gowal (Point 991). The small summit cairn lies 50m off-path to the right.

Another short descent of 30m/100ft and re-ascent of 80m/250ft puts you atop ▲Cairn Bannoch, a small rocky outcrop set in a rolling sea of greenery. Distances and height differentials are not great on this part of the White Mounth.

Cairn of Gowal   CAIRN BANNOCH   Creag an Dubh-loch

BROAD CAIRN

If you have climbed Creag an Dubh-loch and Cairn of Gowal, two of the four subsidiary Tops of Broad Cairn and Cairn Bannoch, why not bag the remaining two? ΔCraig of Gowal is the rise south of the saddle between Cairn of Gowal and Broad Cairn. Surprisingly, it is lower than the saddle itself (!) but it rises a whole 23m/76ft above a lower saddle and sports a lochan on its flat summit.

Not to be outdone, the big flat mound of ΔFafernie, just east of Cairn Bannoch, stands barely 10m/35ft above the intervening saddle. How it has survived for so long in the Tables is a mystery.

Mounth trotters extra: From Fafernie it is only 1½ml/2km north across the plateau to Carn an t-Sagairt Mor (R12; picture on Page 50), and only slightly further south to Tolmount (R9)...

CAIRN BANNOCH

Cairn of Gowal

Alternative Descent via the Dubh Loch
add-on 2ml/3km, 50m/150ft

The easiest way back from Broad Cairn to Loch Muick reverses the outward route, but a return via Creag an Dubh-loch and the shores of the Dubh Loch gives a round trip that maximises views. Note, however, that the descent to the loch is steep, rough and pathless, and it may also require a boots-off stream crossing.

From the saddle between Broad Cairn and Cairn Bannoch, make the short 50m/150ft ascent to the top of ΔCreag an Dubh-loch. The cliff edge east of the summit gives great views of Eagle's Rock waterfall across the Dubh Loch (picture on Page 51). The 60m/200ft fall plunges from the corrie above and is colloquially known as the Piss o' the Coire Boidheach. Even if you choose to return to the Spittal by the ascent track, it is still worth visiting Creag an Dubh-loch for the views.

Over the top, continue in the same north-west direction, descending along the cliff-top around the deep indentation of Central Gully. Stay close to the cliff edge (but not too close!) for continuously exciting views of crag and loch. Eventually you'll reach a stream at the mouth of the corrie on the left. Follow this down to the Allt an Dubh Loch and cross this stream as best you can (it may entail wet feet).

On the far side, a rough path descends past attractive waterslides to the sandy beaches at the head of the loch. You may well wish to spend time here. The loch is well named as its huge flanking crags shade it from sunlight for most of the day.

From the loch, a renovated path descends to Glas-allt-Shiel Lodge on Loch Muick (see Page 59). *En route* it passes some fine pools and runs beneath the attractive Stulan (from the Gaelic *Steallan*, meaning Little Waterfall), which is much more impressive than its name implies.

An estate track runs along the north-west shore of Loch Muick. At the mouth of the loch, a path branches right to rejoin the outward track back to the Spittal.

Creag an Dubh-loch

Dubh Loch

With its 1000m-long, 300m-high wall of immaculate granite, Creag an Dubh-loch lays claim to being the finest cliff face in the British Isles. On each side of the obvious Central Gully, great sweeps of overlapping slabs, pioneered in the 1950s and 1960s, provide testing lines on Central Slabs (left) and Central Gully Wall (right).

▲Carn an t-Sagairt Mor 83 1047m/3436ft

(OS 44, NO 208843) *Carn an Taggersht Moar*, Big Cairn of the Priest (often anglicised to *Carn an Taggert*)

CARN AN T-SAGAIRT MOR

Loch Callater

This quintessential White Mounth dome stands at the north-west edge of the plateau above Deeside. It can be approached from several angles and is close enough to nearby Carn a' Choire Bhoidheach for the two Munros to be climbed together from near Braemar to the north (R13).

For a shorter approach that passes through a whole different landscape, approach from Glen Clunie to the west, where good tracks and paths take you past the scenic shores of hidden Loch Callater.

Morning at Loch Callater

Shortly after the path reaches the shore beyond Lochcallater Lodge, it crosses a spring just before a large shoreline boulder. This is the Priest's Well, named for a priest called Patrick, as is Carn an t-Sagairt Mor and Creag Phadruig above the loch. According to legend it was here one May that his entreaties ended the grip of a long-lasting icy winter by prompting the water to run again.

Carn an t-Sagairt Mor from Glen Callater near Braemar
NO 156882, 10ml/16km, 680m/2250ft

Map note: The summit is on OS 44 but the approach is on OS 43.

Lower Glen Callater

The route begins at the foot of Glen Callater in Glen Clunie, c.2½ml/4km south of Braemar on the A93 (car park with small parking fee). A Land Rover track runs along lower Glen Callater between low hills to Loch Callater, rising only c.130m/400ft in 3ml/5km. The scenery is undemanding, but the riverside track gives a pleasant enough approach walk on a warm, sunny day. It is signposted 'Public Path to Clova' and is the northern section of Jock's Road (see Page 35).

At the mouth of the loch, the track forks in front of Lochcallater Lodge. Go left to a gate in the perimeter fence. The path to Carn an t-Sagairt Mor climbs left beside the fence, but first visit the boarded-up lodge and the stables, now a bothy, for views of the loch. It lacks hillsides of any great interest, but it's a wild spot whose beauty is improved considerably when its waters sparkle in morning sunlight.

Beside the fence, the path climbs straight up the hillside before bearing right at a gentler angle. It has been re-surfaced where it needed to be and is now in excellent condition as it sweeps across the hillside high above

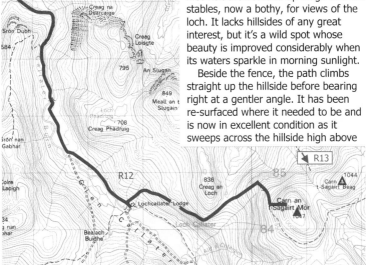

The summit of Carn an t-Sagairt Mor is strewn with the wreckage of an RAF English Electric Canberra that crashed here on a clear night in 1956. The Court of Inquiry was unable to determine the cause of the accident.

You'll find two groups of metal around 100m west of a line between the north and summit cairns. The largest piece of wreckage lies NE of the north cairn, beside the path to Carn an t-Sagairt Beag. Another piece lies buried in the bog on the bealach between the two hills.

Lochcallater Lodge and Stables Bothy

Loch Callater

the loch, with great views of the craggy glen beyond, backed by Tolmount (picture on Page 35).

Above the head of the loch, the path veers left across a bealach then turns right to climb more steeply up Carn an t-Sagairt Mor's north-west shoulder. After reaching a broken fence, it becomes indistinct and, at an old gate, bears right to contour *around* Carn an t-Sagairt Mor. It eventually runs across the White Mount all the way to Lochnagar, but today's objective is fortunately a tad closer.

Quit the path at the old gate and continue up beside the fence on traces of path to reach Carn an t-Sagairt Mor's summit plateau. You arrive on the plateau at the north end, where a cairn highlights the northern view over Deeside to the peaks of the Northern Cairngorms. The ▲ summit cairn lies 100m to the south.

Beyond the summit, the White Mounth stretches into the distance, beckoning. Carn Bannoch (see Page 46) is the nearest Munro... but remember you'll have to come back.

Striding out across the White Mounth   BROAD CAIRN   CAIRN BANNOCH

CARN AN T-SAGAIRT MOR

▲ Carn a' Choire Bhoidheach 42 1110m/3642ft
(OS 44, NO 226845) *Carn a' Chorra Vaw-yich,*
Cairn of the Beautiful Corrie

Creag an Dubh-loch CARN A' CHOIRE BHOIDHEACH Eagle's Rock

Waterfall

Dubh Loch

Viewed from Broad Cairn (R11)

Like neighbouring Carn an t-Sagairt Mor (R12), this is a typical White Mounth swelling whose attractions lie more in the ascent route than in the summit topography. At one time the name White Mounth was used to refer solely to Carn a' Choire Bhoidheach, but it now refers to the whole plateau.

Also like its neighbour, it can be approached from several angles. The time-honoured ascent route begins on Deeside near Braemar to the north. From here, a path climbs all the way onto the White Mounth, topping out at the 962m/3157ft bealach between Carn an t-Sagairt Mor and the lower hill top of Carn an t-Sagairt Beag and giving easy access to the summits.

The approach route gives a steady ascent through Ballochbuie Forest, past Garbh Allt waterfall (*Garrav Owlt,* Rough Stream) and up the hillside known as the Smugglers' Shank, offering extensive views over Deeside to the Northern Cairngorms. Good tracks and paths make the ascent easy and there is much to see along the way, especially in the vicinity of the rocky prow of The Stuic.

Ballochbuie Forest was purchased in 1878 by Queen Victoria to prevent it from being felled. It now forms one of the largest remaining continuous stands of very old Scots pines in the country and is managed solely for conservation purposes.

It is an important breeding ground for ground nesting birds such as black grouse, red grouse and the endangered capercaillie. Since 1998 it has been designated a Special Area of Conservation under the European Habitats Directive.

Carn a' Choire Bhoidheach from Keiloch near Braemar
NO 188912, 12ml/20km, 860m/2800ft

Map note: Most of the route is on OS 44 but the start is on OS 43.

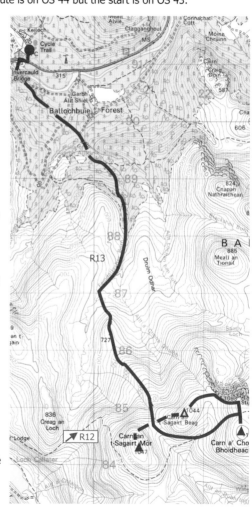

Begin at Keiloch car park, 3ml/5km east of Braemar on the A93 (small fee, 24hr toilet). The car park is situated 200m up a minor road that leaves the A93 150m east of Invercauld Bridge. Walk back to the eighteenth century bridge, cross it and bear left to take the main track through the peaceful pine groves of Ballochbuie Forest.

Ignoring side tracks to left and right, follow the main track across the Glenbeg Burn to a fork just before the Garbh Allt. Branch right here on a track up the stream's right-hand side.

At the next fork, where the right branch descends again into the forest, go left through a gate to keep climbing beside the Garbh Allt. Soon you'll reach a hairpin bend (NO 198896, see opposite) and, a few hundred metres further, another fork. Again go left. At the next and final fork, stay right to avoid crossing the stream.

At the hairpin bend on the Garbh Allt track, a path goes straight on to Garbh Allt Falls, which can just be seen through the trees. The multi-tiered falls have no great volume but you may agree with Queen Victoria that the view from the ornate footbridge over them is 'extremely pretty'. Worth the short side trip. And from there you can climb heathery paths to take a short-cut and rejoin the track higher up (bypassing the fork beyond the hairpin).

The track now bears right to head south up the shallow glen of the Feindallacher Burn. It exits the forest at the upper fence and ends at a corrugated tin shelter used by sheep at NO 204874, around 3ml/5km from the car park.

A path continues, so well-surfaced and finely graded that it is difficult to decide where the approach ends and the climb begins. It crosses the burn, now just a small stream, and climbs the broad tongue of the Smugglers' Shank, with the rounded summits of Carn an t-Sagairt Beag and Carn an t-Sagairt Mor to left and right ahead.

The path becomes indistinct higher up, but you should be able to follow it all the way onto the bealach between the two summits, staying left of a marshy hollow. Keep going until you reach the path that crosses the bealach from right to left.

The round lump of ΔCarn an t-Sagairt Beag blocks the way to Carn a' Choire Bhoidheach. Paths of varying distinctness go over or around it. As there's little to choose between them, we'd go *around* on the way out and *over* on the way back.

Carn an t-Sagairt Beag

CARN AN T-SAGAIRT MOR

The Smugglers'
Shank

The Smugglers' Shank was at one time used to transport illicit whisky over the Mounth from Deeside to all parts south, hence its name.

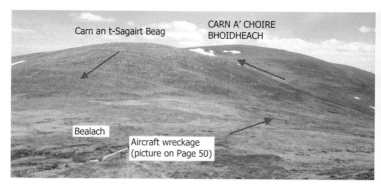

Carn an t-Sagairt Beag

CARN A' CHOIRE
BHOIDHEACH

Bealach

Aircraft wreckage
(picture on Page 50)

Contour around the hillside to pick up the main path across this part of the Mounth, which comes up from Glen Callater (R12). Follow it up onto the broad saddle between The Stuic and Carn a' Choire Bhoidheach, where a small cairn marks the start of a side path to Bhoidheach. The ▲ summit

cairn lies far back on a mossy plateau.

For awesome views on the way back, cross the saddle to the nearby summit of The Stuic, then follow the cliff edge across another saddle to make the short climb over ΔCarn an t-Sagairt Beag and regain the Smugglers' Shank path.

The summit of The Stuic (aka The Stuie), meaning Pinnacle, tops a 180m/600ft-high prow that separates two craggy, lochan-studded basins to the north. Famously, despite his club foot, Lord Byron scrambled up the prow as a 15-year-old in 1803.

LOCHNAGAR

CAC CARN BEAG   Cac Carn Mor

The Stuic

▲Lochnagar — Cac Carn Beag 21 1155m/3789ft

(OS 44, NO 243861) probably from Gaelic *Lochan na Gaire*, Lochan of Laughter or Noise, perhaps referring to the wind among the crags (Sir Hugh preferred the derivation *Loch na Gabhar*, Loch of the Goat)

Viewed from Meikle Pap

LOCHNAGAR

CAC CARN BEAG

Eagle Ridge

Black Spout

England, thy beauties are tame and domestic
To one who has roamed over mountains afar
Oh! for the crags that are wild and majestic,
The steep frowning glories of dark Lochnagar.

Dark Lochnagar
by Lord Byron

This highest Cairngorm mountain south of Deeside is fittingly the most distinguished on the White Mounth. The great crescent of cliffs that encloses its north-east corrie and loch has inspired generations of climbers, hillwalkers, poets, painters and Balmoral royals.

The finely chiselled granite crags can be viewed from several vantage points on the renovated ascent path, which in its final stages runs close to the corrie rim. It is no exaggeration to call the scenery awesome.

Lochnagar was originally known by variant spellings of Beinn nan Ciochan (Mountain of the Breasts), referring to its conical granite tors and highpoints. A direct translation of Cac Carn Beag gives Little Shit Cairn, although Cac is more likely a corruption of Cadha, meaning Steep Place.

One might assume that the habit of referring to the whole mountain by its loch rather than by its summit reflects Victorian prudery but, as evidenced by eighteenth century maps, it began long before that.

Lochnagar from Glen Muick near Ballater
NO 310851, 11ml/18km, 850m/2800ft

Begin at the Spittal of Glenmuick car park, at the end of the Glen Muick road, as for Route 11. Follow the continuing estate track past the visitor centre then turn right on the track signposted 'Lochnagar path' to reach Allt-na-giubhsaich Lodge (*Owlt na Gyoosich*, Stream of the Pines). Take the signposted path through the woods on the right of the lodge. This joins a wider path-cum-track that climbs the glen behind to a low 678m/2585ft pass on Lochnagar's east side (NO 273861).

The Lochnagar path forks left here

Cuidhe Crom

Meikle Pap

Fox Cairn Well

at a conspicuous cairn. It descends 30m/100ft before climbing steadily to the north-east corrie rim. Though somewhat rough and boulder-studded, it has been sufficiently renovated to provide continued easy going.

Meikle Pap

For an unparalleled view of the north-east corrie, make the short detour up the conical outpost of Meikle Pap (*Meikle* is a Scots word meaning *Big*). From the saddle below it, passed on ascent, the summit is only 60m/200ft above. If you fancy a spot of clambering, its summit tors are great fun to explore.

Shortly before the last right-hand bend to the skyline, a small side path runs 30m left to the Fox Cairn Well (NO 263856), a useful water-bottle-refill point on a hot day (easily located by means of an adjacent large boulder with memorial plaque).

The path reaches the north-east corrie rim at a saddle south of ΔMeikle Pap for a first view of the loch and cliffs. It then makes a steeper ascent to a highpoint on the corrie rim. The former eroded path has been replaced by a rocky staircase, known as The Ladder (from Gaelic *Leitir*, Hill-slope), which climbs the bouldery slope.

You emerge onto the extensive summit plateau that extends around the corrie rim and onwards to form the White Mounth. From here on, the ground is littered with flat rocks. The path becomes indistinct in places but the route remains obvious.

A 30m/100ft descent leads to a low point on the rim at the head of the Red Spout, a gritty gully that is one of the corrie's most notable features. The path then veers away from the

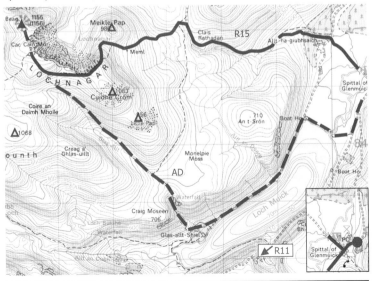

'The jewel of all the mountains here'
(from Queen Victoria's diary, September 6, 1850)

CAC CARN BEAG

Red Spout

rim to surmount a steepening and regain the rim at Cac Carn Mor – a minor rise near the summit topped by a surprisingly large cairn.

Now only a dip of c.15m/50ft

Black Spout Pinnacle

separates you from the pyramid of rocks that forms the summit of ▲Cac Carn Beag. As with Aonach Beag and Aonach Mor in the Central Highlands, *Beag* (little) is higher than *Mor* (big).

Between the two you'll pass the top of the Black Spout, an even bigger gully than the Red Spout. The trig. pillar stands on Cac Carn Beag's topmost boulder, just above a mountain indicator (picture on Page viii).

On descent, make sure at a path junction on Cac Carn Mor that you don't veer right onto a more pronounced path across the Mounth to The Stuic.

While the famous Black Spout is technically an easy rock climb, the whole mile-long crescent of crags sports a variety of challenging routes on impeccable granite. Eagle Ridge is a classic test piece on 250m of superb rock.

Apart from glimpses over the crags, the most knee-trembling sight for rim walkers is Black Spout Pinnacle, which rears up dramatically on the east side of its gully.

Alternative Descent via the Glas Allt
add-on 1ml/1½km, save 60m/200ft ascent

This variation makes a round trip possible and features some fine sections of renovated path beside waterslides, waterfalls and a stream for which the adjective *gurgling* was surely invented. The bottom section is steep and rough but remains safe as long as you don't trip over the edge.

On descent from Cac Carn Mor, the path forks right from the main path after c.600m at an obvious junction (NO 247852). The going alternates between steep stone staircases and gravelly raised sections that are a joy to motor along. The path descends past a considerable waterslide into the 'lost valley' of the Glas Allt (Green Stream), giving wonderful streamside walking across a variety of mosses.

At the end of the valley the path crosses a bridge and reaches the top of a mighty 50m/160ft waterfall (NO 271830), below which Loch Muick resembles nothing less than a Norwegian fjord. Zigzags lead down to the foot of the fall, where on a hot day you can leave the path for a refreshing shower of spray. Further down, another bridge takes you back to the left bank of the stream. Finally a number of paths run through the woods of Glas-allt-Shiel Lodge to the shores of Loch Muick.

Follow the track along the loch's north-west (left-hand) shore then take a path across its mouth to join the far shore track, which takes you back to the car park.

Glas Allt waterfall was a favourite of Queen Victoria and Prince Albert. Following his untimely death, she had Glas-allt-Shiel Lodge built below it in 1869. At its rear (NO 276824) is a bothy maintained by Dundee University Rucksack Club.

▲ **Mount Keen** 235 939m/3081ft
(OS 44, NO 409869) in Gaelic *Monadh Caoin*, Gentle Hill

MOUNT KEEN

This Humble Hump, the most easterly of all Munros, lies far back on the Mounth east of Glen Muick. We have read descriptions of it as a shapely cone, but this is to overstate the case a tad.

The mountain's height and location nevertheless give it commanding views and make any route up its flanking moors of tangled heather seem like a walk on the wild side out of all proportion to the ease of the ascent. And ascents are surprisingly easy, courtesy of the Mounth Road, an ancient cattle droving road, now a rough track, which crosses the shoulder of the mountain to connect Deeside with the coastal plains.

An approach from either end of the track is possible. The southern route from Glen Esk, described here, is much easier and far more popular than the northern route from Glen Tanar. It is shorter, less steep and more scenic, and it boasts an excellent new path.

Mount Keen can be a miserable spot in cloud but go on a fine day and the ascent is surprisingly rewarding.

After the first recorded ascent of a Munro (Stuchd an Lochain) in 1590, the second was of Mount Keen in 1618 by John Taylor, the London 'Water Poet', who composed poems for his passengers as he sculled them across the Thames.

Thanks to his day job, he was able to provide expert testimony when enveloped by wet cloud: 'it yielded so friendly a deaw, that it did moisten thorow all my clothes; where the old proverbe of a Scottish Miste was verified, in wetting me to the skinne.'

Mount Keen from Glen Esk near Edzell
NO 447804, 11ml/18km, 680m/2250ft

The route begins at the end of the minor road along Glen Esk, which leaves the B966 just outside Edzell. From the car park at the road end, walk past the churchyard and turn right on a path signposted 'Public Footpath to Ballater'. This joins a Land Rover track from Invermark Lodge and gives a pleasant 2½ml/4km stroll across the flats of broad-bottomed Glen Mark to the Queen's Well (NO 420829) and Glenmark Cottage.

The Queen's Well

The Ladder

Glen Mark

Beyond the cottage, a stonier track begins the steady ascent to Mount Keen. It zigzags up The Ladder (from Gaelic *Leitir*, Hill-slope) to reach the bleak moors above, then it rises more gently onto the peak's west shoulder.

When you reach a large cairn just around a left-hand bend (NO 405852), leave the track for the obvious path that climbs to the summit. Renovated in the 2000s, this excellently surfaced path now forms a granite grit motorway that is a pleasure to tread (speed restrictions apply on descent).

As an adjective the Gaelic word *caoin* means *kind* or *gentle*, presumably referring to Mount Keen's topography. As a verb it means *to wail* or *to regret*. We trust your experience of the hill is more in keeping with its adjectival connotations.

Queen Victoria drank from the well that now bears her name during an 1861 crossing of the Mounth Road. She found the water 'pure' but it is less so these days. To commemorate her visit, an arched monument, with 6m/20ft buttresses in the shape of a crown, was built over the well. It is not known whether QV made the short detour from the highpoint of the road to the summit of Mount Keen.

MOUNT KEEN

Ladder Burn

The Ladder

After c.350m another path (the continuing Mounth Road) branches left to bypass the summit. Note that older maps do not show recent path re-alignments. On reaching the summit cone, the new path uses stone staircases to surmount bouldery terrain and reach the ▲summit rocks.

The Mount Keen motorway

Both Glen Esk and Glen Mark merit further exploration. A half-hour's walk west of the Queen's Well in upper Glen Mark (N.B. including an easy ford), there's a wonderfully wild spot beneath the rock beehive of Craig o' Doune. There are fine waterfalls here both on the Burn of Doune (NO 401837) and in an intricate little gorge cut by the Water of Mark (NO 394833).

Near the latter is Balnamoon's Cave, where the Jacobite Laird of Balnamoon hid for months following the defeat at Culloden in 1746. Entered by a narrow vertical slit on rocky ground c.23m/75ft above the river, it is as hard to find today as it ever was.

There is also much to see in Glen Esk beyond the car park: ruined Invermark Castle, Loch Lee and, further along, the Falls of Unich and Damff. See notice board at car park. In the lower glen it's worth stopping at the Loups of Edzell to view waterfalls in a wooded gorge flanked by the Rocks of Solitude. Look for a signpost to the latter around a mile from the B966.

▲ **Sgor Gaoith** 36 1118m/3668ft
(OS 36/43, NN 902989) *Skorr Goo-y*, Wind Peak
▲ **Mullach Clach a' Bhlair** 114 1019m/3343ft
(OS 35/43, NN 882927) *Moolach Clach a Vlah ir*,
Summit of the Stone of the Plain (named for a nearby rock outcrop)

SGOR GAOITH

Loch Eanaich

Not the direction of ascent!

To the right (east) of the A9 as it sweeps up Strathspey from Newtonmore to Aviemore, Sgor Gaoith is the highpoint on an undulating ridge that separates Glen Feshie from Gleann Eanaich. The summit cairn teeters on the edge of cliffs that tower 600m/2000ft above Loch Eanaich.

The easiest ascent route begins in the more serene Glen Feshie on the other side of the ridge. Famed for its beautifully wooded central section and canyon-like upper reaches, this is often regarded as the most picturesque of all Cairngorm glens. From the glen, a renovated path climbs to 1030m/3400ft on the plateau south of Sgor Gaoith, putting the summit within easy reach.

Further upglen, a vehicle track climbs to within a few hundred metres of Mullach Clach a' Bhlair, a rounded top on the plateau a few miles south of Sgor Gaoith. For a longer day, the track can be used to give an easy round trip over both Munros.

Sgor Gaoith from Achlean (Glen Feshie)
NN 851984, 10ml/16km, 870m/2850ft

Map note: The whole route is on OS 43 only.

Begin at the car park at the end of the public road on the east side of Glen Feshie, c.800m before Achlean (*Achlain*) cottage. Walk along the road and, at the top of the hill just before Achlean, branch left on a path beside a roadside boulder inscribed 'Carn Ban Mor' (Big White Cairn). The name refers not to the boulder but to the

mountain above, which is one of Sgor Gaoith's five subsidiary Tops.

The path crosses a short stretch of moor to meet another coming up from the cottage and becomes an excellent highway to the heights. It goes through a gate then climbs out of the trees and up the left-hand side of heathery Coire Fhearnagan (*Corra*

The Achlean path

Achlean

Coire Fhearnagan

SGOR GAOITH

Yarnagan, Corrie of the Little Alder Place), so well-surfaced that it's a pleasure to walk (picture on Page xx).

At the 750m contour it reaches a brief levelling, above which it becomes a bit steeper and rougher as it makes its final ascent to the skyline. Easing with height, it

Just beyond the gate on the ascent path, a side path branches right to the Badan Mosach – a series of small cascades on the

Allt Fhearnagan that link to form a 50m/160ft fall. Despite its unfortunate name (meaning Dirty Spot!), it's worth a visit.

curves right towards the Allt Fhearnagan and tops out at a cairn at the 1030m contour on the south shoulder of Carn Ban Mor.

Go left here on a boot-worn path that crosses △Carn Ban Mor's rounded summit, only 20m/60ft above. It becomes lost for a while on the stony summit plateau but soon reappears to descend 40m/150ft to a grassy saddle and make the final110m/350ft climb to Sgor Gaoith's ▲summit.

The abrupt change of scenery at the vertiginous summit, perched high above Loch Eanaich, never fails to startle. Prepare to be awed.

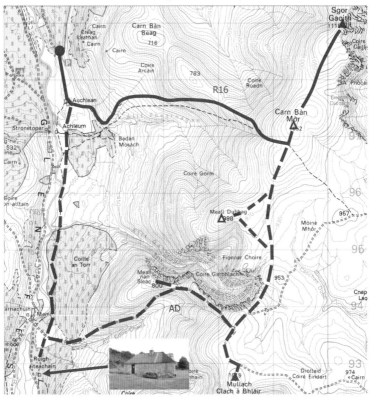

At Sgor Gaoith's summit, look below right on Pinnacle Ridge for the pinnacle of A' Chailleach (*A Chyle-yach*, The Old Woman), then look for her counterpart among the crags on the far side of Loch Eanaich, known as Am Bodach (*Am Potach*, The Old Man). When no-one is looking, they are said to hurl rocks at each other.

Bonus Munro: Mullach Clach a' Bhlair

add-on 5ml/8km, 100m/350ft

The Mullach lies 3ml/5km south across the plateau from the cairn at the top of the Achlean path, but the crossing is easy and a Land Rover track then gives a fast descent. After returning to the cairn from Sgor Gaoith, keep straight on across the plateau, aiming for the low point on the rim at the head of Coire Garbhlach (*Corra Garrav-lach*, Rugged Corrie). The Mullach is the rise on the corrie's far (south) side.

Meall Dubhag   SGOR GAOITH

Coire Garbhlach

MULLACH CLACH A' BHLAIR

As long as you stay right of an extensive area of peat hags, the heath gives good walking almost anywhere, and a number of paths further aid progress. For the best corrie views, make the short detour up ΔMeall Dubhag (*Myowl Doo-ak*, Hill of the Little Dark One), the minor Top on the

MULLACH CLACH A' BHLAIR

Coire Garbhlach

Viewed from the slopes of Meall Dubhag

The 560m/1830ft watershed at the head of Glen Feshie is the lowest between Speyside and Deeside, and the route over it has long tempted road builders. It was surveyed by Wade in the 1730s and Telford in the 1820s, and was even investigated by Inverness-shire County Council as late as the 1960s.

May the route remain forever roadless for future lovers of wild places to enjoy.

corrie's near (north) rim. From here, the rounded hump of the Mullach is seen at its best above the corrie's south-side crags.

Follow the rim around the head of the corrie to reach the vehicle track on the corrie's far side. At a track junction, the right branch descends to Glen Feshie, but first nip up the left branch, which crosses the Mullach close to its summit.

Follow the track to near its high-point, just around a long left-hand bend, where a small cairn marks the start of a path that climbs the final few hundred metres to the ▲ summit.

After retracing steps to the track junction, roll down the Glen Feshie descent track. It may detract from the wildness of the area but it gives a gratifyingly speedy descent. Initially it runs below the rim of Coire Garbhlach to the saddle before Meall nan Steac (*Myowl nan Stachk*, Hill of the Stack), a sentinel above the corrie entrance. Here it leaves the rim to descend to the glen, where it crosses a grassy track on flats just before the former bridge over the Feshie at Carnachuin.

Detour 700m to the left if you want to visit Ruigh-aiteachain bothy, other-wise go right. The track runs through woods to a T-junction. Go right here on a track to the Allt Garbhlach and cross on stepping stones. On the far side a good path continues to Achlean.

Canyon-like Coire Garbhlach is remarkable in having a narrow, winding entrance that hides the 'lost valley' of the wider upper corrie, giving it a pear shape.

The best viewpoint is Meall nan Steac at the corrie entrance. From the saddle where the vehicle track leaves the corrie rim, a good path makes the short ascent.

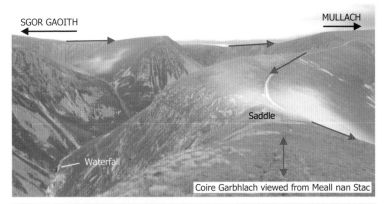

SGOR GAOITH

MULLACH

Saddle

Waterfall

Coire Garbhlach viewed from Meall nan Stac

The prominent chimney stack near Ruigh-aiteachain bothy is all that remains of an 1830s building that was once adorned by deer frescoes painted in situ by Sir Edwin Landseer, famous for his 'Monarch of the Glen' painting. The frescoes have long since gone and, unless preservation plans are realised, the chimney will soon follow.

▲ **The Devil's Point** 130 1004m/3294ft
(OS 36/43, NN 976951) Victorian euphemism for Bod an Deamhain (*Bot an Jevin*, The Devil's Penis)

THE DEVIL'S POINT

River Dee

In the secret heart of the Northern Cairngorms, The Devil lures you into his domain. The arrowhead of The Devil's Point is the most striking peak in the National Park. It looms over the southern entrance to the Lairig Ghru, the great pass that links Aviemore to Braemar, like a guarding sentinel.

Flanked by crags on three sides, it permits easy access only from the saddle that connects it to the high plateau on the west side of the Lairig.

Surprisingly, this saddle can also be reached easily directly from below. From Corrour Bothy, sited in the depths of the Lairig, a path sneaks up Coire Odhar beside the crags to take The Devil unawares.

Of course, first you have to reach the bothy, and this involves a lengthy but scenic approach walk of 8ml/13km each-way. Visiting the heart of the Cairngorms is a privilege that doesn't come without effort.

At the foot of The Devil's Point, Corrour Bothy stands in some of the wildest country in the Scottish Highlands. It is named for the corrie behind it (Coire Odhar, *Corr-oa-ar*, Dun-coloured Corrie). Built in 1877 as a deer watcher's bothy, it was renovated in 2006, complete with an experimental composting toilet.

The Devil's Point from Linn of Dee near Braemar

NO 064898, 18ml/29km, 740m/2450ft
Linn of Dee to Corrour: 8ml/13km each way, out 230m/750ft, back 60m/200ft
 + ascent from Corrour: 2ml/3km, 450m/1500ft

Map note: The whole route is on OS 43 only.

The walk-in to Corrour Bothy at the foot of The Devil's Point is lengthy but progressively scenic. From the back of Linn of Dee car park (toilets; small parking fee), a path joins the Land Rover track up tranquil Glen Lui to Derry Lodge. Just beyond the lodge, cross the Derry Burn by a footbridge and turn left on a path that continues along Glen Luibeg.

The path crosses grassy flats and cuts a scenic swathe through Old Scots Pines, grass and heather to the Luibeg Burn. The pinewood ambience, the ribbon of path, the feeling of venturing into the Cairngorm wilds, the sense of anticipation... all make for a wonderful approach walk.

Nearing the Luibeg Burn, the path forks. Branch left to cross the stream on stepping stones (Luibeg Crossing) or, if the water is high, by a bridge

THE DEVIL'S POINT

Evening in the Lairig Ghru

CAIRN TOUL

Corrour Bothy

Situated amid fine stands of Old Scots Pines, Derry Lodge was built in the 1850s then expanded. In its heyday it played host to guests such as the Prince of Wales (later King Edward VII), who came for the shooting. During World War II it was a military training base, and after that it became a base for the Cairngorm Club, Scotland's oldest climbing club.

It has been empty and boarded-up since 1967 but it remains a listed building. The National Trust for Scotland maintains the exterior shell while discussions about its future use continue.

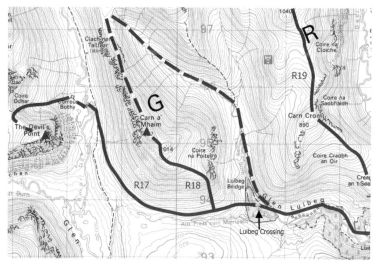

400m upstream. On the far side, the path climbs 230m/750ft around the flanks of Carn a' Mhaim, passing a branch to the summit (R18).

It then becomes more bouldery on a 60m/200ft descent to the bothy, with The Devil's Point looming into view ahead, seemingly impregnable (puns on a postcard, please). As it approaches the River Dee, the path forks. The right branch runs through the Lairig Ghru to Aviemore (see Page 79). Branch left to cross the river (footbridge) to reach the bothy.

The Devil's summit is now only 450m/1500ft overhead and the ascent route is revealed to be little more than a bothy dweller's training exercise. Behind the bothy, on the north side of the summit, a renovated stalkers' path climbs the hillside into Coire Odhar, a shallow bowl of grass and heather with an attractive waterslide at its back.

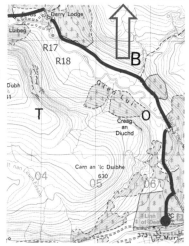

In the corrie, the path crosses the stream and zigzags up more steeply right of the waterslide. Near the corrie rim it traverses back left across the

CARN A' MHAIM

THE DEVIL'S POINT

Coire Odhar

stream and climbs more steeply still to top out on the plateau above. There's a very short section of steep, gravelly ground here, where you may decide to use hands or other parts of the anatomy for security. Extra-sensitive walkers may need encouragement, but it's soon passed.

You emerge onto the plateau at the broad saddle to the north-west of The

Devil's Point, only 700m from the summit. The path forks but you can take either of the two branches as they reunite higher up.

On the final stretch to the summit along the broad, gentle west ridge, the path becomes indistinct on bouldery ground. However, it's not far now to the cliff-edge eyrie and viewpoint that is the Devil's commanding ▲ summit.

Glen Luibeg path   Homeward bound   Glen Lui track

▲ **Carn a' Mhaim** 95 1037m/3403ft (OS 36/43 NN 994951)
Carn a Vaa-im, Breast-shaped Peak (literally Cairn of the Breast; *Mhaim* is the Gaelic genitive of *Mam*)

Carn a' Mhaim stands opposite The Devil's Point at the south end of the Lairig Ghru, the two Munros guarding the gateway to the wilds beyond. Its name reflects its shape when viewed from the south and it is from this side, via the south-east shoulder, that it is most easily climbed.

Point 1014 of CARN A' MHAIM

SE Shoulder

Luibeg Burn

The ascent has one quite steep section, but a renovated path ensures that there is no difficulty. Once up, the views over the Lairig Ghru are superb, and you can explore along the north ridge to enjoy them to the full.

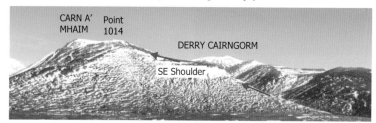

CARN A' MHAIM   Point 1014

DERRY CAIRNGORM

SE Shoulder

Carn a' Mhaim from Linn of Dee near Braemar
NO 064898, 14ml/22km, 680m/2250ft

The approach to Carn a' Mhaim is as for The Devil's Point (R17), following tracks and paths from Linn of Dee to Derry Lodge and Luibeg Crossing (see Page 69 for details).

Once across the Luibeg Burn, follow the path up the far side until it starts to level off after c.500m. Here, at an obvious fork, the renovated Carn a' Mhaim path bears right to climb the steep south-east shoulder.

Rock staircases, built to prevent future erosion, make for a stiff initial 370m/1200ft pull above Luibeg Crossing, so you might want to take it easy for a while. The angle eases at the 800m contour, by which time most of the hard work is behind you.

SE Shoulder · Point 1014 · CARN A' MHAIM · N Ridge

SE Shoulder

A direct line to the summit is blocked by Point 1014, with its carpet of broken boulders. To find easier going, a gritty path bears left around the top to rejoin the skyline at the shallow saddle beyond. This line has the added benefit of taking you to the rim of the Lairig Ghru for dramatic views across its depths to The Devil's Point (R17) and Braeriach (R20). Once on the saddle, Carn a' Mhaim's ▲summit is only 38m/92ft higher.

The map for this route is combined with that for The Devil's Point on Page 70.

Exploration Extra: The North Ridge

Carn a' Mhaim sports one feature unique in the Cairngorms – a scenic high-level ridge that is a pleasure to stroll along. The ridge runs for 1½ml/2½km parallel to the Lairig Ghru and connects the mountain to Ben Macdui's awkward southern slopes via an 800m/2600ft bealach.

Leaving the summit, a gentle descent along a broad crest leads to a brief rocky section. There is no difficulty here, although some may be intimidated by the big drops to either side. Others might even wish it was more exciting!

It's probably not worth going further as the ridge then broadens again and the path descends rubbly slopes to the bealach below Ben Macdui. Over the bealach, the path bears right to climb Macdui's south-west spur but soon comes to an abrupt halt in a massive, steeply-angled boulderfield. Climb Macdui by R22 instead.

Adventurous souls who revel in pathless terrain of heather, clumpy grass and bog can make a round trip back to Luibeg Crossing by descending the deep green glen on the right (east) of the bealach. It is a 2ml/3ml jaunt

BEN MACDUI

BRAERIACH

On the N Ridge

BRAERIACH

Rocky section

down to the mouth of the glen at the confluence with the Luibeg Burn, with a rough little path eventually taking hold on the left bank of the river. The Luibeg Burn is crossed by a boulder-hop or paddle. On the far side, a good path runs a further 1½ml/2km down to Luibeg Crossing.

As an alternative way down from Carn a' Mhaim's summit, the route adds a total of 2½ml/4km to the day.

▲ **Derry Cairngorm** 20 1155m/3790ft (OS 36/43 NO 017980)

from the Gaelic Carn Gorm an Doire (*Carn Gorram an Durra*, Blue Cairn of the Woods, i.e. the Old Scots Pines of Glen Derry). Known historically as An Cairn Gorm but renamed to distinguish it from Cairn Gorm itself

DERRY CAIRNGORM

R19

Coire Sputan Dearg

On its south side, Ben Macdui extends two arms around Glen Luibeg, with a Munro on each arm: Carn a' Mhaim and Derry Cairngorm. Both are terrific viewpoints. While Carn a' Mhaim lies on the western arm and is a superb eyrie above the Lairig Ghru (R18), Derry Cairngorm lies on the eastern arm and provides equally extensive views all round the compass.

The red granite rocks at its conical summit make it an eye-catching objective when viewed on approach. As with neighbouring Carn a' Mhaim, the ascent is initially steep in places but eased by a renovated path.

The summit of Derry Cairngorm is a text-book example of a *felsenmeer* or *blockfield*, in which the bedrock has been weathered and split by frost action into boulders and rubble. Other prime examples are found at the summits of Ben Macdui and Ben Nevis. It is not the easiest terrain to cross but R19 avoids the worst of it.

Derry Cairngorm from Linn of Dee near Braemar
NO 064898, 15ml/24km, 840m/2750ft

Carn Crom

Little Cairngorm   DERRY CAIRNGORM

Creag Bad an t-Seabhaig

The view along Glen Lui

As for The Devil's Point and Carn a' Mhaim, the route begins with a 3ml/5km walk along the Glen Lui track to Derry Lodge and the Derry Burn footbridge (see Page 69 for details). On the far side of the bridge, take the path that goes straight on to climb out of the pine forest and onto the craggy nose of Creag Bad an t-Seabhaig (*Craik Baad an Chevik*, Crag of the Hawk's Place). It's a steep initial 200m/550ft ascent, with the path occasionally resorting to rock staircases, but height is gained fast.

Creag Bad an t-Seabhaig

Derry Burn

Carn Crom

The path above Creag Bad an t-Seabhaig

Carn Crom

High path

Main path

Little Cairngorm

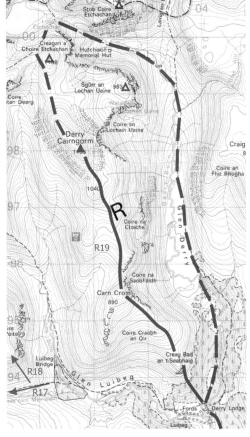

Above here, the angle eases as the path climbs the gentle south-east ridge of Carn Crom (*Carn Crome*, Curved Hill). Nearing the top, you reach a fork. The main path branches right to take a direct line to the bealach beyond, but it crosses a Bad Step (a few steps across sloping rock) that may deter some. If in doubt, take the left branch, which climbs a bit higher to bypass the difficulty. Neither path ventures to the top of Carn Crom itself, although it is a good viewpoint only a few minutes walk away.

Once past Carn Crom, the path continues to climb gently towards Little Cairngorm (OS Point 1040), whose rocky slopes it bypasses on the right. The skyline is regained on the shallow

The map for the approach from Linn of Dee to Derry Lodge is on Page 70.

Little Cairngorm

Viewed from Carn Crom

saddle beyond, leaving a final clamber up boulders to ▲ Derry Cairngorm's short summit ridge. There are two

cairns of apparently equal height, one at each end of the ridge – better touch both to be sure.

The Bad Step (optional)

Summit slopes

It's possible to prolong the scenery by returning to Derry Lodge via Loch Etchachan and Glen Derry. However, the route is 2½ml/4km longer and much rougher. It first descends the boulderfield on the far side of Derry Cairngorm's summit. A path then climbs to the saddle

left of Creagan a' Choire Etchachan and descends to Loch Etchachan on the far side. From here another path runs down Coire Etchachan and Glen Derry to Derry Lodge. It passes some stunning crag and loch scenery, but don't be tempted this way unless you have stamina and experience.

Summit

▲ Braeriach 3 1296m/4252ft (OS 36/43, NN 953999)
Bray-ree-ach, (in Gaelic *Braigh Riabhach*), Grey or Speckled Upland

BRAERIACH

R20

Coire Bhrochain

The great flat summit of Braeriach has more presence than any such summit has any right to have. The summit cairn stands at the edge of Coire Bhrochain, whose seemingly vertical 230m/750ft crags rival those of Lochnagar (Route 14) for spectacle.

No guidebook to the Munros of the Cairngorms would be complete without a route up Braeriach, yet all ascent routes are steep and rough. The easiest approach, described here, has no technical difficulty whatsoever, but it requires fitness and determination on ascent and stamina on descent. It

may not be the longest route in this book, but it may be the most tiring.

The most well-known ascent route begins at the Sugarbowl car park on the Coire Cas road above Aviemore, but this involves negotiating the boulder-jam of the Chalamain Gap both on the outward and return trips. The route described here is 1½ml/ 2½km longer each way and begins 150/500ft lower, but it avoids the Chalamain Gap and actually involves less ascent. It joins the Sugarbowl route in the jaws of the Lairig Ghru, where the main ascent begins.

The Lairig Ghru, which separates the Braeriach–Devil's Point plateau from the Cairn Gorm–Ben Macdui plateau, is one of the Cairngorms' great passes, linking Aviemore to Braemar.

It is more properly the Lairig Dhru (its north-side stream is the Allt Druidh), but

the local pronunciation *Lahrik Ghroo* must have fooled mapmakers. The name is probably derived from the Gaelic Drudhadh, meaning Flowing or Oozing Pass, rather than Ghruamach, meaning Gloomy or Forbidding Pass, although this often seems more apt.

Braeriach from Whitewell near Aviemore
NH 912587, 15ml/24km, 1100m/3600ft

From Whitewell, at the end of a minor road from Coylumbridge just outside Aviemore (signposted Blackpark), the Sugarbowl route can be joined by following the northern section of the Lairig Ghru path.

The Lairig Ghru path in Rothiemurchus Forest

From the road-end car park, descend a 200m path to join a track that runs for 800m to a crossroads. Turn left to follow the track across the Cairngorm Club Footbridge to a junction (NH 938075). The Lairig Ghru path, signposted 'Rothiemurchus path', turns right here. Most of it has been upgraded and the pine forest is a joy to walk through, although there are some short rough sections once the trees are left behind.

The path eventually runs beside the Allt Druidh through a deeply incised glen at the foot of Sron na Lairige (Nose of the Pass). The Sugarbowl path joins from the left and, around 100m further, the stream disappears

underground. At a fork just beyond here, the Braeriach path branches right to climb steeply to a terrace where the Sinclair Hut used to stand before it was demolished in the 1990s.

Ahead now is the steepest part of the route, up the long northern shoulder of Sron na Lairige. The path here has been improved, but its high-stepping rock staircases and slippery gravel chutes will not be to everyone's taste and require care on descent.

Around 350m/1150ft above the Lairig, the angle eases and the path becomes indistinct on rubbly ground. Another steeper section follows, topping out near the rounded summits of ΔSron na Lairge and its north top.

Sron na Lairige

Lairig Ghru

Braeriach is on both OS 36 & OS 43, but the complete route is only on OS 36.

A path contours around the summit itself to avoid a descent on the far side. On grassy ground, the path then gives good, almost level going for a while (at a fork, branch right to stay on the main path).

You are now reaching the heart of the scenery, with the southern view opening up along the Lairig to the great portal framed between Carn a' Mhaim and The Devil's Point. The path descends 30m/100ft to a saddle and continues as a gravelly highway to the rim of Coire Bhrochain, where the view expands across the vast floor of An Garbh Coire (The Rough Corrie) to Cairn Toul and Sgor an Lochain Uaine,

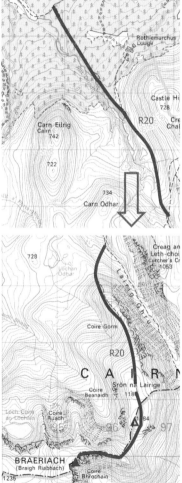

On Sron na Lairige

Coire Bhrochain has so many promontories and indentations that you'll be spoiled for photogenic compositions. The sun hits the cliffs in the morning, so start early.

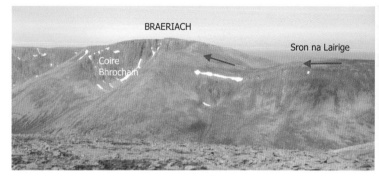

two awkward Munros sporting a lochan in the hanging corrie slung between them.

The remainder of the route is to be savoured. Just follow the obvious trail up around Coire Bhrochain's rim above increasingly awesome cliffs. Braeriach's ▲ summit cairn is perched spectacularly right at the cliff edge.

▲ Cairn Gorm 6 1244m/4081ft (OS 36, NJ 005040)
in Gaelic Carn Gorm (*Carn Gorram*, Blue Peak),
named for its blue tinge when viewed from a distance

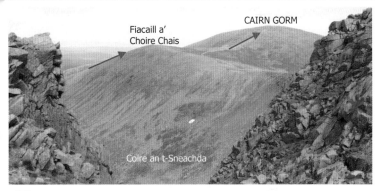

Fiacaill a' Choire Chais

CAIRN GORM

Coire an t-Sneachda

Cairn Gorm's height, prominence, accessibility and fame make it an unmissable attraction. Not only is it one of Scotland's nine 4000ft Munros, but it has given its name to the whole range of mountains behind it. Its big, bouldery summit dome is featureless apart from the large summit cairn, the (locked) mountain rescue hut and the weather station. The skiing infrastructure of Coire Cas (*Corra Cas*, Steep Corrie) below the summit further detracts from the scenery. But the mountain is big enough to rise above these handicaps.

West of Coire Cas lie two more unsullied corries that boast superb crag and lochan scenery: Coire an t-Sneachda (*Corra an Drechka*, Snowy Corrie) and Coire an Lochain (*Corra an Lochin*, Corrie of the Lochan). The three corries together, known as the Northern Corries, sport a variety of mix-and-match routes up and down Cairn Gorm that, thanks to the 630m/2050ft starting point of Coire Cas car park, are surprisingly accessible.

The route described here climbs the west rim of Coire Cas and descends the east, making a circuit that crosses the summit and visits the 1007m/3600ft-high Ptarmigan Restaurant.

The Automatic Weather Station at Cairn Gorm summit, run by Edinburgh's Heriot-Watt University, provides wind speed and temperature data every half-hour. Updates are regularly posted on the internet. Check for current status at: www.phy.hw.ac.uk/resrev/weather.ht

A record wind speed of 173mph was recorded here in March 1986. In December 2009 a reading of 194mph was taken at the entrance to the funicular tunnel just below the Ptarmigan Restaurant, but no recording was made and officially the previous record still stands.

Cairn Gorm from Coire Cas near Aviemore
NH 989060, 4½ml/7km, 620m/2050ft

From Coire Cas car park above Aviemore, a good path climbs the ridge that forms the right-hand (west) rim of Coire Cas. Signposted Coire Cas Mountain Path, it begins on the right of the stream behind the day lodge and climbs to the Ptarmigan service track. Turn right here and walk up the track to just round the second left-hand bend. Here, the path branches right up the hillside onto the broad crest of the upper ridge. Higher up, long series of rock steps ease progress over bouldery and gravelly terrain.

A large cairn signals your arrival on the Cairn Gorm–Ben Macdui plateau at a minor highpoint named Fiacaill a' Choire Chaish (*Fee-acil*, Tooth).

An indistinct path continues left to cross a minor dip and climb 110m/350ft up steepish, gravelly slopes to Cairn Gorm's ▲ summit.

The standard route

The Marquis Well route

Ptarmigan

The map for this route is combined with that for Ben Macdui on Page 90.

The Ptarmigan   CAIRN GORM

The Windy Ridge path

Two paths descend the 150m/500ft slope on the far side of the summit to the Ptarmigan. The standard route goes straight down, following a line of cairns and a steep, rope-lined, 'cobbled' section. For a more congenial route, look further right, below the weather station, to find a better path that curves down less steeply. At the 1190m contour, on a right-hand bend, you'll pass the spring known as the Marquis Well. At the Ptarmigan you can stop at the café and even take the train down if you wish.

On the far side of the building, a track begins the descent of the ridge that forms the east rim of Coire Cas, known as Sron an Aonaich (*Strawn an Eunich*, Nose of the Point). After a short distance, leave the track on a right-hand bend for a path that carries straight on down the ridge.

Named Windy Ridge Path for the benefit of tourists, this well-manicured new path descends the broad crest of the ridge, finishing off with long series of steep stone steps that take you back down to the car park.

The Marquis Well at NJ 007043 is a spring named for the Earl of Huntly, who is said to have drunk its waters when he and his men were pursuing the Earl of Argyll's forces westwards after routing them at the Battle of Glen Livet in 1594.

Alternative Ascent via Coire an Lochain west rim
add-on 2½ml/4km, 190m/600ft

Days on Cairn Gorm are short, so for a better appreciation of what the mountain has to offer, consider a roundabout approach to the summit. This route up the right-hand (west) rim of Coire an Lochain is the most scenic as it follows the skyline of all three Northern Corries.

From Coire Cas car park, take the path that contours right (south-west) round the foot of Fiacaill a' Choire Chais. Ignore all left branches and keep to the well-surfaced main path as it climbs steadily up the far rim of Coire an Lochain to reach grassy flats west of Cairn Lochan.

Cairn Lochan

The path continues to Ben Macdui (R22), but leave it to climb over ΔCairn Lochan. A rough path climbs right then back left to ease the angle on the 150m/500ft ascent. Once up, you'll obtain amazing cliff-edge views of Coire an Lochain, whose lochan nestles at the foot of mighty crags.

Cairn Lochan

grassy flats

Fiacaill a' Choire Chais — CAIRN GORM — Stob Coire an t-Sneachda — Cairn Lochan

Over the top of Cairn Lochan, follow the cliff edge along the corrie rim, descending past the top of the jagged ridge that divides Coire an Lochain from Coire an t-Sneachda and offers scramblers a challenging ascent route to the plateau.

A dip is crossed and easy slopes of grass, gravel and boulders rise to ∆Stob Coire an t-Sneachda, with yet more thrilling views over that corrie's lip to lochans far below. Over the top, a good path right of the cliff edge takes you to Fiacaill a' Choire Chaish (or around it) to join R21 for the final rise to ▲Cairn Gorm.

> The cliffs of Coire an Lochain resemble giant natural masonry, block-faulted into titanic towers and gullies. The most prominent feature is a swathe of pink granite known as the Great Slab. Snow compacts here to form a unique glacier, complete with crevasses. In Spring this avalanches onto the ground below.

The Funicular Railway

The funicular was opened in 2001 after years of argument about its environmental impact. Planning permission was eventually agreed only on condition that walkers be banned from using it. Anyone who takes the train up will not be allowed outside the Ptarmigan top station at 1097m/ 3600ft, with its shop, café, exhibition and outside viewing terrace.

Not surprisingly, such constraints reduced income, and the funicular was taken into public ownership in 2009 with the aim of increasing 'the numbers of non-skiing visitors'.

There is now a Walkers' Entrance by which you can enter to use the facilities and optionally take the train down. Since 2010 it has also been possible to pay for a guided walk to Cairn Gorm summit.

For details of times, prices, facilities etc. visit www.cairngormmountain.org.

▲ Ben Macdui 2 1309m/4296ft (OS 36/43 NN 989989)

Possibly from the Gaelic Beinn na Muic Duibhe (Mountain of the Black Pig) but more likely from Beinn MhicDhuibhe (MacDuff's Mountain). Macduff was a Thane (clan chief) of Fife who owned the land.

BEN MACDUI

R22

Lairig Ghru

Ben Macdui's ranking as Scotland's second highest mountain makes it a popular objective. As with Cairn Gorm, the summit dome itself lacks shapeliness, but the peak's central position at the heart of the Cairngorms gives it all-round views that make the cairn a difficult spot to leave.

From Coire Cas, the Cairn Lochan path (R21 Alternative Ascent) reaches the Cairn Gorm–Ben Macdui plateau equidistant between the two Munros. The remainder of the route to Macdui develops into a wild and atmospheric sky-high walk with superb views across the trench of the Lairig Ghru.

The view from Macdui's summit is as extensive as befits such a height. Peaks can be picked out with the aid of a mountain indicator, erected by the Cairngorm Club in 1925. For unobstructed views, spend a while wandering around the rim of the summit dome. Especially riveting, if you boulder-hop a few hundred metres to the west, is the close-up view across the Lairig Ghru into the depths of An Garbh Coire and surrounding 4000ft peaks such as Braeriach and Cairn Toul.

In swirling cloud, Ben Macdui's summit plateau is an eerie place. It is said to be haunted by Am Fear Liath Mor (The Big Grey Man), a malevolent spectral apparition it would be prudent to avoid.

Spine-chilling encounters have been reported by several notable mountaineers. Eminent Victorian Alpinist Norman Collie famously fled the summit in panic when he heard giant footsteps behind him.

Ben Macdui from Coire Cas near Aviemore
NH 989060, 10ml/16km, 680m/2250ft

Map note: The whole route is on OS 36 only.

From Coire Cas car park, take the excellent path up the west rim of Coire an Lochain, described as R21 Alternative Ascent (Page 86). Beyond the head of the corrie, the path crosses an almost level expanse of grassland before climbing again across the west shoulder of Cairn Lochan.

grassy flats

As you climb, look for a cairn that marks a short detour on the right to a tremendous viewpoint over the Lairig Ghru to Cairn Toul.

Viewpoint view

CAIRN TOUL

SGOR AN LOCHAIN UAINE

Lairig Ghru

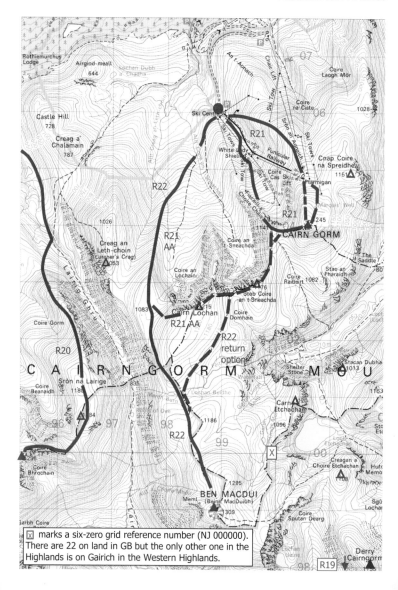

⊠ marks a six-zero grid reference number (NJ 000000).
There are 22 on land in GB but the only other one in the
Highlands is on Gairich in the Western Highlands.

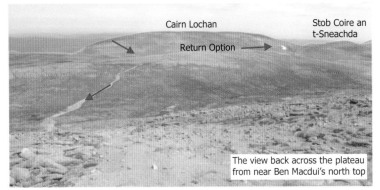

Cairn Lochan

Stob Coire an t-Sneachda

Return Option ⟶

The view back across the plateau from near Ben Macdui's north top

After crossing the shoulder, the path descends 40m/140ft to a saddle, where it passes between Lochan Buidhe (*Lochan Boo-ya*, Yellow Lochan) and a smaller lochan, the former draining west to Loch Avon and the latter east to the Lairig Ghru. Situated at the heart of the plateau, Lochan Buidhe is the highest lochan in the country and, even on a cloudless day, feels like a very remote spot.

The path now climbs again into a boulderfield, where cairns mark the line to take. At a larger cairn, another cairned line joins from Lochan Buidhe (see Return Option overleaf).

Thankfully the boulderfield soon ends and from here on the walk becomes easy again, on a gritty path across bare terrain. It crosses a level section, makes a short ascent, levels off again to contour around Macdui's rounded north top, and finally rises onto the ▲ summit boulder-dome.

North top   BEN MACDUI

Return Option

Lochan Buidhe

The final stretch

BEN MACDUI

In 1847 the Royal Engineers ('Sappers') lived for a time at the summit to conduct a trigonometrical survey. The remains of their bothy can still be seen c.150 south-east of the summit.

Numerous stone bivouacs stand as testament to nights spent here by soldiers on training exercises during World War Two. Around 300m north-west of the summit is a small memorial to a plane that crashed here during another exercise.

The Sappers' Bothy

Return Option

If a return trip across the plateau to Ben Macdui is insufficient to exhaust your store of energy, why not bag Cairn Gorm on the way back?

From Lochan Buidhe, a good path contours across the south-east slopes of Cairn Lochan to the rim of Coire an t-Sneachda to join R21 Alternative Ascent. This will add 1ml/1½km and 260m/850ft to the trip.

Return Option

CAIRN GORM

Lochan Buidhe

▲ Bynack More 54 1090m/3577ft (OS 36, NJ 041063)

Bynack Moar, Big Bynack: Bynack could be derived from *Beinneag* (meaning little mountain – Big Little Mountain!), *Beannag* (meaning coif or cap – Big Cap), *Binneag* (meaning roof-ridge of a house) or Ben Eag (Mountain of the Notch). Also known historically as Caiplich (*Caaplich*, Place of Horses)

Bynack Beag — BYNACK MORE — A' Choinneach

Loch Avon

This detached Munro is one of the Cairngorms' loneliest mountains, hidden from the madding crowd behind Cairn Gorm, from which it is separated by the V-shaped defile of Strath Nethy. Unusually for the Cairngorms, it is so surrounded by deep glens that the summit looks conical from some angles.

Close up, things get even more interesting as the summit slopes are adorned with granite 'barns' (tors) that form boulder playgrounds. To add to this, nearby A' Choinneach is an incomparable viewpoint over the Cairngorms' wildest spot – the Loch Avon basin. In all, Bynack More is a seductive Munro whose ascent will give you an insight into why the Cairngorms backcountry attracts so many devotees of wilderness.

The easiest ascent route approaches the summit via the Pass of Ryvoan and the Lairig an Laoigh. Like its neighbour the Lairig Ghru on the west side of Cairn Gorm–Ben Macdui plateau, the Lairig an Laoigh (Lahrik an Loo-y, Pass of the Calves) is a great north-south pass on the east side. Its northern section reaches a height of 790m/ 2600ft on Bynack More's shoulder and gives easy access to the summit.

Bynack More from Glenmore Lodge near Aviemore
NH 991097, 14ml/22km, 780m/2550ft

The route begins at Glenmore Lodge, reached by a short road from Glenmore Visitor Centre near Aviemore. There are parking spaces just beyond the lodge. From here, the Lairig an Laoigh runs through the remarkably flat Pass of Ryvoan to round the northern outliers of Cairn Gorm and reach the foot of Bynack More.

BYNACK MORE
Bynack Beag

A first view of Bynack More across Strath Nethy

The route begins as a wide and smoothly surfaced track that conducts tourists to An Lochan Uaine at the heart of the pass. A rougher track then continues to a fork. Ryvoan Bothy lies around 600m along the left branch (signposted Nethy Bridge), while the route to Bynack More branches right (signposted Braemar).

The track becomes even rougher as it climbs slightly around the foot of Cairn Gorm's long north ridge and ends at the site of Bynack Stable at the foot of Strath Nethy (NJ 021105). The corrugated iron shelter that used to stand here was blown down in January 2005 but the wooden bridge over the River Nethy still stands.

Across the river, the Lairig an Laoigh continues as a renovated and well-graded path that climbs across Bynack More's heathery northern shoulder and down into the glen on the far side. At its 790m/2600ft highpoint, it crosses the foot of the north ridge. Leave it here for another, obvious path, still being improved, that climbs directly to the summit.

The Lairig an Laoigh path above Bynack Stable

The summit ridge is crested by a jumble of small granite outcrops that, should the urge strike you, are great fun to clamber over. Beside them, a fringe of gentle grass slopes carries easy paths for those who disdain such superfluous expenditure of energy.

Looking back down Bynack More's north ridge

The ▲ summit used to be hidden among the topmost outcrops and frustratingly hard to find, but it now sports a fittingly large cairn.

Before leaving the summit, you may wish to go take a look at the two groups of monolithic tors known as the Barns of Bynack and the Little Barns of Bynack, which stand only a short distance away down the south ridge like a natural Stonehenge.

To the north, an extensive northern panorama stretches to the horizon over the forests and plains of Strathspey, but the gaze of the true aficionado of wild places will be drawn southwards into the mountainous heart of the Cairngorms.

The Barns

With energy replenished from a sojourn at the Barns, consider a longer side trip to A' Choinneach, the flattened rise seen to the south-west. The intervening grassy saddle gives excellent walking and the expansive view over remote Loch Avon from the summit plateau is simply superb.
Return trip: 3ml/5km, 120m/400ft.

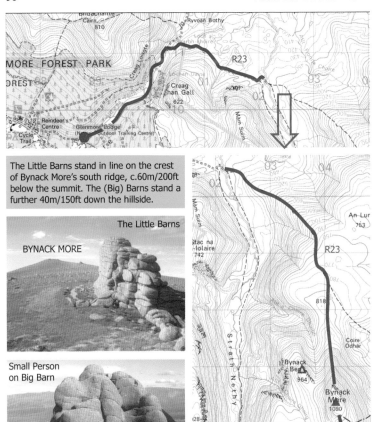

The Little Barns stand in line on the crest of Bynack More's south ridge, c.60m/200ft below the summit. The (Big) Barns stand a further 40m/150ft down the hillside.

The Little Barns

BYNACK MORE

Small Person on Big Barn

The Pass of Ryvoan is a picturesque, pine-studded defile that cradles the deep emerald pool of An Lochan Uaine (*An Lochan Oo-anya*, The Green Lochan). The lochan has two remarkable characteristics:

it has no visible outlet and it is frequented by fairies. Proof of the latter claim lies in the water's saturated colour, which results from the elusive creatures' penchant for doing their laundry here.

▲ Beinn a' Bhuird 11 1197m/3928ft (OS 36, NJ 92006)

Ben a Voorsht (often anglicised to *Voord*), Table Mountain. Bhuird is the genitive of the Gaelic word Bord, meaning Board or Table.

BEINN A' BHUIRD

Viewed from Deeside

I n its own idiosyncratic way, the summit of Beinn a' Bhuird is as amazing a spot as the summit of Skye's Inaccessible Pinnacle... and as different from it as imaginable. As though giving a two-fingered salute to the pointy-peaked spotlight grabbers of the west coast, its summit plateau is so flat that for 2ml/3km it varies in height no more than a few tens of metres, and that mostly in one spot.

There is no place in the Highlands that gives such a feeling of having strayed onto an island in the sky. Which is not to say there's no vertical stuff to admire. While western slopes drop away tamely, the eastern side is scalloped by a trio of craggy corries.

The mountain's remoteness makes it a real prize, yet the route to the summit is surprisingly easy, thanks to an excellent path that is a rewilded former vehicle track. It's a long hike, up convex slopes that hide the retiring summit for most of the ascent, but take it steady and you'll get there. The angle is gentle and the path does eventually take you along the rim of the eastern corries for some startling views on a singular mountain.

Beinn a' Bhuird has always divided opinion among those who have climbed it. In 1810 the Rev. George Keith belittled it as 'an immense mass, without beauty or fertility'.

In 1819 naturalist William MacGillivray considered the summit to be 'the most noble without exception which I had ever seen'. You decide.

Beinn a' Bhuird from Linn of Quoich near Braemar
NO 118911, 18ml/28km, 870m/2850ft

From the foot of the mountain it is 5ml/8km to the summit, but to that must be added a 4ml/6km walk to the foot along a Land Rover track on the west side of the Quoich Water.

From roadside parking at Linn of Quoich, at the road end 10ml/16km beyond Braemar, a path climbs to join this track. The walk-in would be a pleasant riverside walk through the pine trees were it not for the need to get some miles beneath the boots.

Carn Allt na Beinne

BEINN A' BHUIRD over here

Mountain biking the approach track from Linn of Quoich

It is 4ml/6km to the flats where the Quoich Water is joined by the Allt an Dubh Ghlinne (River of the Dubh Ghleann, *Doo Glen*, Black Glen). This can be crossed on stepping stones if the water is low, otherwise it will require a paddle. The track ends soon afterwards in a fine stand of pines at the foot of Carn Allt na Beinne, an outlying point on Beinn a' Bhuird's southern slopes. Beyond here, the track has been rewilded.

The gritty new path climbs out of the trees and round the flanks of Carn Allt na Beinne into the deep heathery glen of the Alltan na Beinne (Streamlet of the Bens). Here it climbs diagonally up the left-hand hillside at a steady angle to reach a shallow dip on the skyline known as An Diollaid (*An Jee-alitch*, The Saddle). The old shelter marked on the map just above the dip is today only a windbreak.

Now begins the climb up Beinn a' Bhuird's south-west shoulder. Views south and west are extensive but unfortunately too distant to distract from the task at hand.

Beinn a' Bhuird is on OS 36, but OS 43 is needed in addition for the approach track.

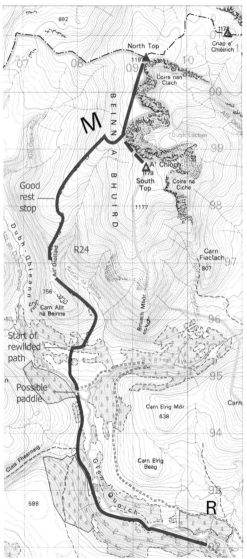

A levelling at the 940m contour (NO 076981) makes a good rest stop, with the remainder of the route to the summit plateau now visible at last and good views opening up west into the heart of the Cairngorms.

On terrain of grass, boulders and rubble, the path tackles the final bulge of mountainside and reaches a point just below the skyline at NO 085993, where the old track ended. Here it turns sharp right before climbing back left (the path that goes straight on is a rubbly short cut).

You reach the skyline just above the low point on the rim of Coire an Dubh Lochain, the middle of Beinn a' Bhuird's three great eastern corries. The sudden reveal of the huge bowl comes as a scenic jolt after the tame approach. The Dubh Lochan (*Doo Lochan*, Black Lochan) is the largest of several seen in the corrie depths.

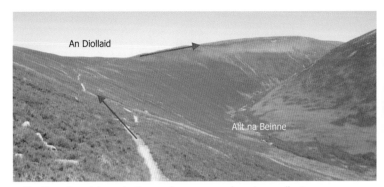

An Diollaid

Allt na Beinne

For the return trip, note the marker cairn a few metres short of the rim. Off-route to the right, and worth the side-trip if you have the energy (perhaps on the return trip?) are the ∆South Top and the rocky eminence of A' Chioch.

Turning left, make a beeline for the summit. Paths struggle to make an impression on the grass-and-gravel terrain of the plateau, but the going everywhere is excellent.

Cross a small rise to reach the rim of Coire nan Clach (Stony Corrie), which is even larger than Coire an Dubh Lochain. Here you'll pick up a more distinct path that curves around the rim to Bhuird's ▲summit. The summit cairn inhabits an extraordinary, flat wilderness of scrub that makes a suitably surreal spot to contemplate the mountain's startling contrasts.

Approaching the plateau

There have been attempts over the years to turn Braemar into an Aviemore-like ski resort. Developments for the winter of 1932 included a toboggan run, a skating park and a curling rink... then no snow fell.

In 1963 a vehicle track was bulldozed up the south-west flank of Beinn a' Bhuird to open up Coire Gorm for ski development. Lack of snow again thwarted the venture.

After purchasing the mountain in 1995, the National Trust for Scotland rewilded the track and replaced it with the current path. On the ascent to An Diollaid, Coire Gorm is the steep corrie across the glen.

A' Chioch

Coire an Dubh Lochain

Summit

Coire nan Clach

Summit

Quoich (*Coo-ich*, Quaich or Cup) is named for the Punch Bowl, a (now broken) pothole carved out by the Quoich Water. According to legend, the Earl of Mar literally filled it with punch for his men to toast the beginning of the 1715 Jacobite rebellion.

For a pleasant short walk, wander up the east-side path (on the right-hand side of the river), past the waterfalls of the Linn and the Punch Bowl itself, to the bridge at NO 101922.

For an alternative start (or end) to R24, a path climbs from the bridge to join the west-side track.

▲ Ben Avon — Leabaidh an Daimh Bhuidhe 17

1171m/3843ft (OS 36, NJ 131018) *Ben Ahn*, probably named for the River Avon (from the Gaelic Abhainn, meaning River). Other possible derivations include Ath Fhionn (Fair River, named for Fingal's wife, who legend says drowned in it) and Ath Fionn (Ford of the Fingalians, i.e. the Fords of Avon upriver). Ben Avon refers to the whole mountain. The actual summit is named Leabaidh an Daimh Bhuidhe (*Lyeppy an Dev Voo-ya*, Bed of the Yellow Stag).

BEN AVON
northern corries

Ben Avon is a sprawling mountain mass whose summit is only one granite tor among many that dot the outstretched summit plateau and its bulging shoulders. Not only does it have four current subsidiary Tops, but it also has six additional deleted Tops that, were they still extant in Munro's Tables, would see it reign supreme as King of the Tops. It is such a complex mountain, so replete with widely paced features of interest, that no single approach can do it justice.

The shortest approach is from Deeside to the south, but even that is a very long hike with a rough final climb. In any case, it is on a northern approach that the mountain shows its best features, with a 3ml/5km plateau walk that links tor to tor above the wild corries of upper Glen Avon.

No guidebook to the Cairngorms would be complete without Ben Avon but, if ever a mountain was both easy and tough, this is it. You'll need stamina and good routefinding ability to climb it. The miles are long and the trail intermittent. The walk-in to the foot of the mountain follows a private road along the serene glen of the River Avon for 7½ml/12km. It's a beautiful riverside walk, but be prepared for it to seem even longer on the way back. Is it worth it? Of course it is.

Ben Avon from Tomintoul NJ 165176

Walk-in (or ride-in by mountain bike): 7½ml/12km each-way
Ascent from Glen Avon: 10ml/16km, 830m/2700ft (Total mileage: 25ml/40km)

The route begins at the Queen's View car park on the outskirts of Tomintoul. To find the car park, go south along the main street, past the A939 turning, and turn right along the road signposted Delnabo. The paved road continues beyond the car park as a private road along Glen Avon.

From the car park, the walk-in to Ben Avon begins on a vehicle track that rejoins the glen road at a bridge just over a mile away. After 450m the track passes the Queen's View, beloved of Queen Victoria, where a mountain indicator helps you pick out the distant summit plateau of Ben Avon, peeking above nearer hills.

Once you reach the road, follow it up the broad green glen, with its snaking river, lush riparian scenery and Rhine-like vistas. All that's needed to complete the image is an occasional hill-top *schloss*.

The tarmac ends 5½ml/9km from the car park, leaving a further 1½ml/2km of Land Rover track to Inchrory Lodge, a grand Victorian building still well used during the sporting season. Follow the track around the lodge to a junction at the confluence of the River Avon and the Builg Burn. Turn right here over the Builg Burn bridge and reach a junction with a rougher track after 300m.

The day's main ascent begins here, 7½ml/12km from the car park, but the good news is that it's now only 440m/1450ft up to the start of the fun.

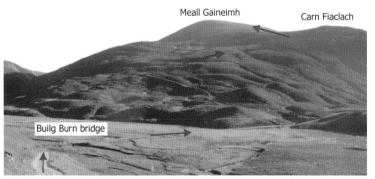

Meall Gaineimh

Carn Fiaclach

Builg Burn bridge

The River Avon flows down from scenic Loch Avon, which occupies a craggy basin on the remote south-east side of Cairn Gorm. The river's legendary clarity results from a lack of peat in its catchment area.

Fingal's wife is not the only one to have been misled by its deceptive shallowness. As the old rhyme has it:
    The Water of Avon, it runs sae clear,
    'Twad beguile a man o' a hundred year.

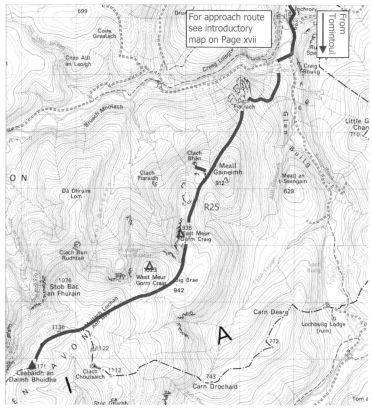

Clach Bhan (Clach Vahn, Stone of the Women) is the most fascinating of all Ben Avon's tors and demands a short detour as it lies only a couple of minutes off-path. Nooks and crannies abound. After rain, secret rocky grottos fill with water to form perfect paddling pools. The flat top, reached by a short clamber, is pock-marked with curious chair-like hollows. Until the late 19th century, pregnant women would visit them in the belief that it would ensure an easy birth.

Clach Bhan   Meall Gaineimh →

The rough track climbs part way up the hillside ahead, aiming for Meall Gaineimh (*Myowl Gahny*, Sandy Hill), the highpoint seen above. When it ends, a rough path continues. If you lose it in the heather, just keep going until you find it again. After skirting Carn Fiaclach (Toothed Cairn) it becomes indistinct on gravelly ground as it seeks to skirt Meall Gaineimh's summit. At this point, aim for the prominent cairn seen on the skyline to the right to find it again.

From the cairn, a good path runs between Meall Gaineimh and a tor-crowned hillock on the right. Further right is Clach Bhan (see opposite). You have now reached the plateau, which runs for 3ml/5km to Ben Avon's summit, and are entering tor country.

Ahead now is the tor-studded summit ridge of ΔEast Meur Gorm Craig (East Blue Finger Crag). The path contours below the crest to reach the bealach beyond, which separates it from its twin ΔWest Meur Gorm Craig. Many find the short clamber to East Meur Gorm Craig's summit tors an irresistible diversion.

On the far side of the bealach, climb a short rise to find the continuing path, which contours above a large tor-lined corrie on the right to reach a shallow grassy ravine formed by

East Meur Gorm Craig

Summit   Point 1136

a stream. The path disappears here but can be found again as it crosses the ravine from left to right.

At the end of the ravine you emerge onto moorland, with the prominent tor of Clach Choutsaich (named for Clan Coutts) visible on the skyline ahead. The path, very indistinct at first, goes diagonally right, parallel to a more prominent stream on the left. It disappears occasionally but can be followed up to the bealach on the far side of West Meur Gorm Craig. It disappears for good here, but the going remains good on boulder-strewn grass and turf.

Go straight up the hillside ahead to reach a higher level of plateau, then stay on the high ground as it leads you from tor to tor, eventually arcing left over Point 1136 (not sharp left to Carn Choutsaich) to Ben Avon's ▲ summit.

The summit tor is the second highest on the mountain and feels as though it's a long way from anywhere (there's a good reason for this!). The 15m/50ft ascent to the top, beginning at a notch on the north side, is easier than it looks. More of a clamber than a scramble, it may nevertheless prove a tad too airy for some.

Now... that's half the walk done. Time for the minor matter of the return trip.

The summit tor from the west

The summit tor from the east

INDEX

Loch Eanaich

Braeriach summit plateau from Sgor Gaoith

Luath Press Limited

committed to publishing well written books worth reading

LUATH PRESS takes its name from Robert Burns, whose little collie Luath (*Ga*
swift or nimble) tripped up Jean Armour at a wedding and gave him the chance
speak to the woman who was to be his wife and the abiding love of his
life. Burns called one of 'The Twa Dogs' Luath after Cuchullin's
hunting dog in Ossian's *Fingal*. Luath Press was established
in 1981 in the heart of Burns country, and now resides
a few steps up the road from Burns' first lodgings on
Edinburgh's Royal Mile.
Luath offers you distinctive writing with a hint of unex-
pected pleasures.

Most bookshops in the UK, the US, Canada, Australia,
New Zealand and parts of Europe either carry our
books in stock or can order them for you. To order direct from
us, please send a £sterling cheque, postal order, international
money order or your credit card details (number, address of
cardholder and expiry date) to us at the address below. Please add
post and packing as follows: UK – £1.00 per delivery address;
overseas surface mail – £2.50 per delivery address; overseas
airmail – £3.50 for the first book to each delivery address, plus £1.00 for each
additional book by airmail to the same address. If your order is a gift, we will happ
enclose your card or message at no extra charge.

Luath Press Limited
543/2 Castlehill
The Royal Mile
Edinburgh EH1 2ND
Scotland
Telephone: 0131 225 4326 (24 hours)
Fax: 0131 225 4324
email: sales@luath.co.uk
Website: www.luath.co.uk